PUFFIN

HANS ANDERSE

HANS CHRISTIAN ANDERSEN (1805–75) was born in Odense, Denmark, the son of a poor shoemaker and a washerwoman. As a young teenager, he became quite well known in Odense as a reciter of drama, and as a singer. When he was fourteen, he set off for the capital, Copenhagen, determined to become a national success on the stage. He failed miserably, but made some influential friends in the capital, who got him into school to remedy his lack of proper education. He hated school: aged seventeen, he was in a class of twelve-year-olds and was constantly mocked by them and by the teachers.

In 1829 his first book – an account of a walking trip – was published. After that, books came out at regular intervals. At first, he considered his adult books more important than his fantasies. In later life, however, he began to see that these apparently trivial stories could vividly portray constant features of human life and character, in a charming manner. There were two consequences of this. First, he stopped regarding his stories as trifles written solely for children; second, he began to write more original stories, rather than retelling traditional tales.

He once said that ideas for stories 'lie in my mind like seeds and only need the kiss of a sunbeam or a drop of malice to flower'. He would often thinly disguise people he liked or disliked as characters in his stories: a woman who failed to return his love becomes the foolish prince in 'The Little Mermaid'; his own ugliness and humiliation, or his father's daydream of being descended from a rich and powerful family, are reflected in 'The Ugly Duckling'.

Hans Andersen's stories began to be translated into English as early as 1846. Since then, numerous editions, and more recently Hollywood songs and a Disney cartoon, have helped ensure the continuing popularity of the stories in the English-speaking world. But nothing matches the charm of the written stories, a dozen of which are freshly translated into modern English in this volume.

Some other Puffin Classics to enjoy

ALADDIN AND OTHER TALES FROM THE ARABIAN NIGHTS
SINDBAD THE SAILOR AND OTHER TALES FROM THE ARABIAN NIGHTS
N. J. Dawood

GRIMM'S FAIRY TALES
Brothers Grimm

A TRANSLATION
WITH INTRODUCTION AND NOTES
BY NAOMI LEWIS

Hans Andersen's Fairy Tales

Illustrated by

PHILIP GOUGH

PUFFIN

For Kaye Webb

PUFFIN BOOKS

Published by the Penguin Group
Penguin Books Ltd, 80 Strand, London WC2R 0RL, England
Penguin Group (USA), Inc., 375 Hudson Street, New York, New York 10014, USA
Penguin Books Australia Ltd, 250 Camberwell Road, Camberwell, Victoria 3124, Australia
Penguin Books Canada Ltd, 10 Alcorn Avenue, Toronto, Ontario, Canada M4V 3B2
Penguin Books India (P) Ltd, 11 Community Centre, Panchsheel Park, New Delhi – 110 017, India
Penguin Group (NZ), cnr Airborne and Rosedale Roads, Albany, Auckland 1310, New Zealand
Penguin Books (South Africa) (Pty) Ltd, 24 Sturdee Avenue, Rosebank 2196, South Africa

Penguin Books Ltd, Registered Offices: 80 Strand, London WC2R 0RL, England

www.penguin.com

First published in Puffin Books 1981
This edition published in association with the Danish Tourist Board 2004
1

Set in 12/15 pt Monophoto Plantin
Made and printed in England by Mackays of Chatham plc

British Library Cataloguing in Publication Data
A CIP catalogue record for this book is available from the British Library

ISBN 0-141-31955-0

Contents

Acknowledgements

I wish to express particular gratitude to the late Marianne Helweg for her valuable help and advice on points of Danish, and to Kaye Webb, who originated this book and continually encouraged it on its course. And appreciation and thanks to Doreen Scott for her calm and unfailing patience, and her inspired eye for seemingly vanished manuscripts.

INTRODUCTION

What is genius? Where does it come from? Nobody knows. But it is the nearest thing to magic that any human creature can possess. The young Hans Christian Andersen possessed it, no doubt about that. A penniless boy, growing up in a small far northern land, whose language was scarcely known outside its borders, he was to become the best-known, best-loved Dane in all the world, and so he has remained. In this book are some of the tales that made him so.

Hans Andersen (1805–75) was born in a very poor home in Odense, Denmark. He was later to speak of his life as 'a fairy tale', but this did not mean that success came soon, or easily, or in the way he hoped. Every wish has its price: that's the rule, in fairy tale as in life. Andersen, on his road to fame, had to face as many forests of thorn, steep glass mountains and fearsome trials as any hero of legend.

Still, he was not without a few grains of luck at the start. For one thing, he was an only child. This gave him more chance of not being pushed out into some harsh trade, and of having his parents' attention, his father's especially. These parents were totally unalike except in their love for their son. But both were to influence him, though differently, for the rest of his life.

The mother was a peasant woman, simple and superstitious. Like many of the poor, she could not read. She was terrified of questioning the Church or the Bible or the rights of her wealthy feudal superiors. The father, by contrast, was a natural student and thinker, a man of ideas, a reader of literature. By trade he was a shoemaker. He had no great taste or talent for the job, but then, he had never been given any choice. His free-thinking views on religion and social matters (which today would not be thought odd at all) alarmed and shocked his wife; but she always respected his wish that Hans Christian, unlike himself, should never be forced into work of the wrong kind. Meanwhile, he would take the boy into the woods and point out the grass and flowers and insects, each with a life of its own. He read to him, plays and stories; he made him toys, and the best of these was a toy theatre. The whole world seen in miniature was to be the special mark of Andersen's work.

When Hans Christian was eleven his father died, still a young man, but worn out by hardship and failure. His imagination, his restlessness, his dreams all lived on in his son. So did his mother's superstition, her belief in magic and her sturdy peasant endurance. An odd mixture! But all were part of his nature and his tales.

Odense, where he grew up, was a town like a small story-book kingdom. It contained a royal castle, and many old buildings which live again in the stories. There was also a theatre which attracted the boy irresistibly. As for the people of Odense, they stayed in their rigid stations – nobility, gentry, those in professions, in trade, and last, the labouring poor. No one presumed to step out of place except the washerwoman's crazy boy (as he was now considered). Against all the unspoken rules he was drawn to the thinking and well-spoken, to writers and painters, actors and scholars; some of them lent him books and helped him in small ways.

Yet dreaming, reading and working at his toy theatre could not earn him a living. And so, at fourteen, he set out to seek his improbable fortune in the capital city of Copenhagen. There he was, half-starved, in outgrown clothes, knocking at the doors of likely people, pleading, singing, clowning his way into their attention, into the Royal Theatre and out of it – still seeing himself as an actor, singer or dancer. Oddity though he was, he continued to catch the puzzled aid of patron after patron, scholars, singers, councillors, even royalty itself. Something had to be done with him, that they all agreed. And so, at seventeen, he was sent away to school to make up the education he had missed, Latin, Greek, mathematics and the rest, a great tall scarecrow among the little eleven-year-olds. Worse still (though unknown to his guardians), he lived in dreadful conditions, starved and tormented. It was the darkest period of his life.

But at length the ordeal was ended, the highest examinations were passed, and he was allowed to choose what he wished to do. He chose to write. By the time he was thirty he was an accepted Danish author, with poems, plays, a travel book and a new long novel behind him. He did not expect much interest in a tiny paperback book of his that came out in May of that year, 1835: *Fairy Tales Told for Children*. There were four tales in the book; one was 'The Princess and the Pea' which you will find here. However, there *was* some interest, and a second booklet followed in December. (This is where 'Thumbelina' first appeared.) 'Orsted says,' Andersen wrote to a friend, 'that the fairy tales will make me immortal, for they are the most perfect of all my writings. But I myself do not think so.' Orsted (a leading Danish writer) was a better judge than Andersen. The stories began to excite an ever wider public of adults and children alike; nothing of their kind had been seen before. Their fame spread far beyond Denmark; the first English translation appeared in 1846. Every new set of tales was awaited eagerly, each year, for the rest of his life. By his own count there were 156 at the end. But he had long ceased to use the words 'Told for Children' on the cover; the tales were for everyone.

How do Andersen's stories differ from the traditional tales that we know through Grimm and others? For they do differ, even when they seem to have the same kind of plot. In the folk tale, everyone's path is laid down; you can scarcely ever distinguish witch from witch, prince from prince, goosegirl from yellow-haired goosegirl. In Andersen, though, not only the people and animals are very much themselves, but the same holds for *things* – toys, furniture, flowers, bits of glass, torn paper. And there is more to discover than this.

At first we read for the story. What will become of Thumbelina? Where is little Kay? Which will the goblin choose? But presently we realize that we have been on a journey with a very unusual guide. For a start there is the landscape itself, the woods and meadows, dunes and marshes, the sea (never far off in an island kingdom), the castles, houses, hovels. Like invisible guests we enter these places; we witness the busy human day and then the life that starts when the humans sleep. All of Andersen's Denmark, modern and bygone, man-world and elf-world, is in these tales. Yet how easily the *real* scene leads into fairy tale; the river, so clear and pretty, speeding through fresh green meadows, is taking little Gerda into witch-country, into eerie forests with ruined castles (the haunt of robber bands), into a quest that leads to the coldest place in story, to the northern edge of the world.

The tales have a further interest, especially for sleuthlike readers. In one guise or another

Andersen himself may be found in almost every one, perhaps in a sly detail, perhaps (as in 'The Ugly Duckling', Andersen's own life-tale) through the whole course of the story. There he is in a china sweep who could just as easily be a prince, in a tin soldier born at a disadvantage but with high hopes and dreams, in any poet or student or teller of tales. Wherever there is a paper dancer or paper castle we know whose hand is behind it; Andersen's skill in making these lovely fragile things with his large pair of scissors (first learnt as a child with a toy theatre) can rarely have been matched.

The tales are at their best when read just as they left Andersen's hand, not turned into films or plays. Good as these often are, they miss the vivid, personal telling – the unmistakable voice of the spellbinder. Often, as in 'The Snow Queen', one of the great invented fairy tales of the world, episodes and phrases can stay in the mind for life, each one a talisman: Kay's great flight with the Queen; the dreams rushing past on the stairs; the reindeer ride into regions north of north; the sense of spring after winter, when Gerda steps into the boat for a journey strange beyond all imaginings; the autumn moment when Gerda breaks the rusty lock and leaves the garden of perpetual summer. (It is hard to think of any other work that pictures the seasons with such intense effect – except, perhaps, *Wuthering Heights*.) As for the pieces of ice that refuse to form the needed word, these time and again come to mind when a sentence is hard to write or a problem hard to solve. The pieces *can* fall into shape, that much we know. This story can be read again and again, and give back more every time. *

Andersen stood between two worlds, the old and the new, and both stirred his writer's gift. Horseback and stagecoach were the only means of travel when he was a boy; he lived into a time when railway journeys, telegraph messages and photography were commonplace. Indeed, he was fascinated by all such inventions – perhaps because they extended the range of magic. Is this why science fiction is so much read today? In one curious tale, 'The Millennium' (1853), he imagines the world a thousand years hence. 'The young citizens of America will fly through the air, cross the great ocean, to visit old Europe . . . They will have telegraphed ahead for their hotel reservations . . .' And all will be seen in a week. Not a bad guess – except that his fancies would be fact in much less than a century.

Now for the choice of stories in this book. The main great Andersen tales are here, for a start: some long, some short, they can never be met too often, nor found too late. Among those in the small space left I have included a sparkling story not so often found in selections, 'The Goblin at

* See also Notes on 'The Snow Queen', p. 190.

the Grocer's', and a little tale, 'Dance, Dolly, Dance', that I have never seen anywhere but in the collected works. As a very late work it must have missed the translators.

So many noted writers have been influenced by Andersen that we probably do not realize how greatly original he was. In his own day this was very much easier to see, and is one of the many reasons why even kings and princes made him an honoured guest, and would listen again and again to his tales; why in countries all over the world he was so much valued by adults and children alike. Many today know his tales without even knowing the name of their author – and that's fame too! Sometimes on the tiny scale of the toy theatre, sometimes ranging the ocean, sky and earth, he brings into his stories as much of human life as the reader cares to find. Once you step wholly into the tales he can give you, if you take it, just what the Snow Queen offered Kay – the whole world, let alone a new pair of skates.

NAOMI LEWIS

The Princess and the Pea

There was once a prince who wished to marry a princess – but a real princess she had to be. So he travelled all the world over to find one; yet in every case something was wrong. Princesses were there in plenty, yet he could never be sure that they were the genuine article; there was always something, this or that, that just didn't seem as it should be. At last he came back home, quite downhearted, for he did so want to have a real princess.

One evening there was a fearful storm; thunder raged, lightning flashed, rain poured down in torrents – it was terrifying. In the midst of it all, someone knocked at the palace door, and the old King went to open it.

Standing there was a princess. But, goodness! What a state she was in! The water ran down her hair and her clothes, through the tips of her shoes and out at the heels. Still, she *said* she was a real princess.

'Well, we'll find out soon enough,' the old Queen thought. She didn't say a word, though, but went into the spare bedroom, took off all the bedclothes, and laid a little pea on the mattress.

Then she piled up twenty more mattresses on top of it, and twenty eiderdowns over that. There the Princess was to sleep that night.

When morning came, they asked her how she had slept.

'Oh, shockingly! Not a wink of sleep the whole night long! Heaven knows what was in the bed, but I lay on something hard that has made me black and blue all over. It was quite dreadful.'

Now they were sure that here was a real princess, since she had felt the pea through twenty eiderdowns and twenty mattresses. Only a real princess could be so sensitive.

So the Prince married her; no need to search any further. The pea was put in the museum; you can go and see it for yourself if no one has taken it.

There's a fine story for you!

Thumbelina

Once upon a time there was a woman who wanted a little tiny child of her own, but she didn't know how to set about finding one. So off she went to an old witch and said to her, 'I would so much like to have a little child! Couldn't you tell me where to get one?'

'Oh, that's not difficult,' said the witch. 'Here's a barleycorn for you – and it isn't the kind that grows in the farmer's field, nor the kind that the chickens eat, either. Just put it in a flower pot, and you shall see what you shall see!'

'Oh, thank you!' said the woman, and she gave the witch a silver coin. Then she went home and planted the grain. She hadn't long to wait before a fine big flower sprang up; it looked like a tulip, but the petals were tightly closed as if it were still a bud.

'What a lovely flower!' said the woman, and she kissed the shut red and yellow petals. The moment she did so, the flower burst open with a loud crack. It was a real tulip – you could see that now – but right in the middle of the flower, on the green centre, sat a little tiny girl, graceful and delicate as a fairy. She was no more than a thumb-joint high, and so she was called Thumbelina.

She was given a walnut shell, beautifully polished, as her bed; she lay on a mattress of deep-blue violet petals, and a rose petal was her eiderdown. There she slept at night, but in the daytime she played upon the table, where the woman had put a soup-plate of water with a circle of flowers round its edge, the stalks facing the centre. Floating in the plate was a large tulip petal on which Thumbelina could sit and row from one side to the other, using two white horse-hairs as oars. It was the prettiest sight! She could sing too, in the tiniest, sweetest voice ever heard.

One night, as she lay in her beautiful bed, a toad came hopping into the room through a broken window pane. The toad looked very big and wet as she thumped down on to the table where Thumbelina lay fast asleep under her rose petal.

'Now, *there* be a handsome wife for my son!' said the toad. And she took the walnut-shell bed in which the little girl was sleeping, and hopped with it through the window and down into the garden. At the end of the garden flowed a wide stream, but at the edge it was marshy and thick with mud; this was where the toad lived with her son. He was not at all handsome; in fact, he looked just like his mother. 'Croak! Croak!

Brek-kek-kex!' That was all he would say when he saw the pretty little girl in the walnut shell.

'Don't speak so loudly, or she'll wake,' said the old toad. 'She could still escape from us, for she's as light as a piece of swansdown. I know – we'll put her out in the stream on one of the great water-lily leaves; she will think it an island, for she is such a tiny wisp of a creature. While she is there, we can start preparing the best room under the mud, where you two will make your home together.'

Out in the stream grew a great many water-lilies, with wide green leaves that looked as if they were floating free on the water. The leaf that lay furthest out was also the biggest of all, and that was where the old toad set down the walnut shell with Thumbelina inside. The poor little creature woke up very early the next morning; when she saw where she was, she began to cry bitterly, for there was water all round the big leaf, and no possible way of getting back to land.

Meanwhile, the old toad stayed down below in the mud, busily decorating the room with rushes and yellow water flowers to make it look nice and bright for her new daughter-in-law. Then she swam out again, this time taking her son, to the leaf where Thumbelina was waiting. They had come to fetch the pretty walnut-shell bed so that they could put it in the bridal bedroom before the little bride arrived. The old toad, while still in the water, made a deep bow to Thumbelina, and said:

'This is my son; he is going to be your husband, and the pair of you will live very happily in a fine home down in the mud.'

'Croak, croak! Brek-kek-kex!' was all that the son could say.

Then they took the elegant little bed and swam off with it, while Thumbelina sat all alone on the green leaf, crying, for she had no wish to live with the old toad and to have her son for a husband. Now the little fishes, swimming below in the water, had seen the toad and had heard what she said, so they thrust their heads up, to see the little girl for themselves. But as soon as they did so, they realized how lovely she was, and it grieved them to think that she had to go and live in the mud with the toad. No, that must never happen! So they gathered together in the water round the green stalk of the leaf that she was on, and gnawed and gnawed it through.

Off went the leaf, floating along the stream, carrying Thumbelina far, far away, where the toad could not follow.

On and on she sailed, and the birds in the trees sang out, 'What a pretty little creature!' as they caught sight of her. Further and further along glided the leaf – and that was how Thumbelina journeyed into another country.

A lovely white butterfly kept fluttering round her, and at last it alighted on the leaf, for it had taken a fancy to the little girl. How happy she was now! The toad could no longer reach her, and everything was beautiful, wherever she looked. The water, where the sun shone, was just like gleaming gold. Thumbelina took her sash and gave one end to the friendly butterfly and tied the other to the leaf; now she sped along even more swiftly.

Just then, a big cockchafer-beetle came flying by; he saw the little girl, and in a flash he grasped her slender waist in his claws and flew up with her into a tree. The green leaf went floating on down the stream and the butterfly with it.

Goodness! how frightened poor Thumbelina was when the cockchafer carried her off into the tree! And she grieved, too, for her friend, the white butterfly. But the beetle cared nothing about that. He alighted on the largest green leaf of the tree and set her down, and gave her honeydew from the flowers to eat, and told her that she was very pretty, though not in the least like a cockchafer.

Presently, all the other cockchafers that lived in the tree came to call on her. They looked at her, and the young lady cockchafers shrugged their feelers and said, 'But she has only two legs, the miserable little insect!' 'She hasn't any feelers!' 'Her waist is so thin – ugh! She looks quite like a human! How ugly she is!' That's the sort of thing they went on saying – and yet Thumbelina was really the prettiest little creature.

The cockchafer who had carried her off thought this, certainly, but when all the other beetles declared that she was a fright to look at, he too began to think her ugly, and at last would have nothing more to do with her; she could go wherever she chose. Several beetles flew down from the tree with her and put her on a daisy; there she sat and wept because she was so ugly that the cockchafers would have nothing to do with her – and yet she was the most beautiful little thing you could imagine, lovelier than the most perfect of rose petals.

All through the summer poor Thumbelina lived quite alone in the great forest. She wove herself a bed out of blades of grass, and hung it like a hammock under a large dock leaf as shelter from the rain. For her food, she gathered honey and pollen from flowers, and she drank the dew which lay every morning on the leaves. So the summer and autumn passed; but then came winter, the long cold winter. The birds that had sung so delightfully now flew far away; the trees lost their leaves, the flowers withered. Then the big dock leaf, which had been her roof, curled up and shrivelled, until nothing was left of it but a dry yellow stalk. Thumbelina was terribly cold, for her clothes were all in rags, and she was so fragile and small. It seemed that she would soon be frozen to death. The snow began to fall, and every snowflake that fell on her was as heavy as a shovelful thrown on one of us. After all, she was only an inch high. So she wrapped herself in a withered leaf, but that did not warm her, and she shivered more and more.

By this time she had wandered to the edge of the forest. Just outside lay a large cornfield, but the corn had long been gathered, and now only the bare dry stubble stood up out of the frozen ground. For her, this was like a forest to travel through, and oh, oh, oh! – how she shook with the cold. And then she came to a field-mouse's door, which led to a little house under the stubble. There the field-mouse lived, snug and comfortable, with a store-room full of corn, a warm kitchen and a dining-room. Poor Thumbelina stood at the door like any little beggar-girl and asked if she might have a piece of barley seed, for

she had had nothing at all to eat for the past two days.

'You poor little thing!' said the field-mouse, for she was a kind old creature at heart. 'Come into my warm kitchen and have something to eat with me.' She enjoyed Thumbelina's company, so presently she said, 'You are welcome to stay with me for the winter, only you must keep my place nice and clean, and tell me stories; I am very fond of stories.' Thumbelina did what the good old field-mouse asked, and the time passed happily enough.

'We shall soon be having a visitor,' said the field-mouse. 'My neighbour comes to visit me every week. His house is even better than mine; he has such fine large rooms, and he wears such a handsome black velvet coat! If you could only get him for a husband you would be well provided for. But his sight isn't good. You must be ready to tell the best stories you know.'

Thumbelina did not like the thought of this. She had no wish to marry the wealthy neighbour; he was a mole, and he came to call in his black velvet coat. The field-mouse reminded Thumbelina how rich and learned he was; she told her that his house was twenty times as big as the one that they were in, that he knew about many, many things, though he did not care for the sun and the beautiful flowers, for he had never seen them. Thumbelina had to sing for him, and she sang, *I had a little nut tree,* and *Ladybird, ladybird, fly away home*. The mole fell in love with her because of her sweet voice; but he kept this to himself, for he was a very cautious man.

He had recently dug himself a long passage through the earth linking his own house to theirs, and he gave Thumbelina and the field-mouse leave to walk through whenever they wished. But he begged them not to be afraid of the bird that lay in the passage. He told them that the bird was quite unmarked and uninjured, with all its feathers and beak; it must have died quite recently, with the coming of winter, and had somehow fallen into his underground path.

Then the mole took in his mouth a piece of rotten wood (for that glows just like a fire in the dark) and went ahead to light the long dark passage for his guests. Soon they came to the place where the bird was lying, and the mole thrust up his broad nose against the roof and pushed through the earth, so that there was a hole to let in the daylight. And there could be seen a swallow with its beautiful wings pressed close against its sides, its legs and head huddled into its feathers; the poor bird must surely have died of cold. Thumbelina felt so sorry for it; she loved all the little birds that had sung and twittered to her so delightfully all the summer long. But the mole pushed the swallow aside with his short legs, and said:

'There's one that we shan't hear whistling any more! What a fate to be born a little bird! Thank heaven none of my children will ever be one. A bird can do nothing but say tweet-tweet and then starve to death in the winter.'

'Yes, you have a point there,' said the field-mouse. 'What has a bird to show for all its tweet-tweet-tweet when winter comes? It starves and freezes. And yet everyone thinks so highly of them.'

Thumbelina said not a word, but when the others had moved on she bent down, gently parted the feathers on its head, and kissed its closed eyes. 'Perhaps,' she thought, 'this is the one that sang to me so sweetly during the summer. What happiness it gave me, that dear little woodland bird!'

Then the mole stopped up the daylight hole in the roof and escorted the ladies home. But that night, Thumbelina could not sleep at all, so she got out of bed, and plaited a coverlet of hay; this done, she carried it along and spread it over the bird. At its side she laid some soft thistledown which she had found in the field-mouse's living-room, so that it might rest warm in the cold earth. 'Farewell, you pretty little bird,' said she – 'farewell, and thank you for your lovely song in the summer, when the trees were green, and the sun shone so joyfully on us all.' And then she laid her head on the bird's heart – but at once she felt greatly startled, for it seemed as if something was knocking inside. It was the bird's heart, beating. He was not dead; he was only numb with cold, and now that he had been warmed he began to revive.

In autumn the swallows all fly away to warmer lands. But if one of them is delayed, the cold can freeze its life away; it falls to the ground, and is soon buried under the snow.

Thumbelina trembled with shock; the bird was so much larger than herself, for she was only an inch high. But she gathered her courage and tucked the thistledown closer round the poor bird, and then ran back for her own bedcover, a mint-leaf, to place over his head.

The next night she crept out again to visit him – and now he was certainly alive but so weak that he could only open his eyes for a moment to look at Thumbelina. There she stood with a piece of rotten wood in her hand, for she had no other lantern.

'Thank you, thank you, pretty little girl,' said the sick swallow. 'You have warmed me so well that I shall soon be strong again, and fly in the bright sunshine.'

'Oh,' said Thumbelina, 'it is still cold outside – snow and frost everywhere. Stay in your warm bed meanwhile, and I shall take care of you.'

Then she brought the swallow some water in a leaf, and the bird drank, and told her how he had injured one of his wings on a thorn bush and so had not been able to fly as fast as the other swallows when they journeyed to warmer lands. At last he had fallen to the ground, and remembered no more; he could not imagine how he had come to be where he was lying now.

All through the winter the swallow remained in the passage. Thumbelina looked after him and grew very fond of him. But she said nothing of this to the mole or the field-mouse, for they did not care for birds. At length, the spring came, and the sun's rays began to pierce through the earth. The swallow said good-bye to Thumbelina and re-opened the hole that the mole had made in the roof of the passage. The sunshine filled them both with joy, and the swallow asked Thumbelina to come away with him; she could sit on his back, and they would fly far off into the leafy greenwood. But Thumbelina knew that the old field-mouse would be upset if she left like that.

'No, I cannot come,' she said.

'Then farewell, farewell, you kind pretty girl,' said the swallow, and he flew out into the sunshine. Thumbelina watched him soar into the sky, and her eyes filled with tears, for she had become very fond of the poor swallow.

'Tweet, tweet!' sang the bird, and flew off into the leafy wood.

Thumbelina was now very sad. She was not allowed to go out into the bright daylight, and in the field where they lived the corn grew so tall that for her it was like a forest towering overhead.

'You must get your trousseau ready this summer,' said the field-mouse, for their neighbour, the mole with the velvet coat, had made Thumbelina an offer of marriage. 'You must have clothes both of linen and wool, and plenty of blankets and sheets when you are the wife of the mole.'

Thumbelina had to work hard with her spindle, and the mole hired four spiders to weave for her, night and day. Every evening, he would pay them a visit, and every time he would say that when the summer was over, and the sun was not so dreadfully hot, and had stopped baking the earth as hard as a stone, then they would have the wedding. But Thumbelina was not at all happy, for she did not care for the pompous old mole. Every morning, when the sun rose, and every evening, when it set, she would creep outside; when the wind blew the ears of corn apart, she could see the blue sky, and she thought each time how beautiful and bright it was in the open air. She wished so much to see her dear swallow again, but he did not come back; he had flown away into the green and leafy wood.

When autumn came, the whole of Thumbelina's trousseau was ready. 'In four weeks' time,' said the field-mouse, 'you shall have your wedding.' But Thumbelina wept, and said that she did not want to marry the mole.

'Nonsense!' said the field-mouse. 'Don't be so difficult. You are getting a splendid husband. Why, the queen herself has not such a fine black velvet coat. And think of his well-stocked kitchen and cellar! Be thankful for your good fortune.'

And so the wedding day arrived. The mole had already come to fetch Thumbelina; she was to go and live with him, deep under the earth; she would never be able to go up into the radiant sunshine, for the mole could not stand the light. Full of grief, she went to say a last good-bye to the glorious sun; she had always been allowed to come to the doorway, at least, while she was living with the field-mouse.

'Farewell, bright sun!' she said, holding up her arms towards it, and she walked a few steps into the open world. The corn had been harvested and now only the stubble was left. 'Farewell, farewell,' she said again, and she threw her arms around a little red flower still growing among the stalks. 'If ever you see the swallow again, tell him I send my love.'

At that very moment she heard a sound – 'Tweet, tweet!' – exactly overhead. It was the swallow. How glad he was to see his Thumbelina! And then she told him that on this day she had to marry the mole, and go to live in a dark house under the earth, where the sun never shone. And the tears rained from her eyes at the thought of it.

'The cold winter is coming on,' said the swallow. 'I am flying far away to the warm countries. Won't you come with me? You can sit on my back, and tie yourself on with your sash; then we shall leave the mole and his dark house and fly far far away over the mountains to a land where the sun shines even more beautifully than here, where it is always summer, and the groves and trees are full of the loveliest flowers. Ah, come with me, dear little Thumbelina, you who saved my life when I lay frozen in the dark passage under the earth.'

'Yes, I will go with you,' said Thumbelina. She seated herself on the bird's back and tied her sash to one of its strongest feathers. And then the swallow soared high up into the air, over forest and lake, over great mountains where the snow always lies. The frosty air made her shiver, but she crept under the bird's warm feathers, and just peeped out to gaze at the wonderful scenes below.

At last they came to the warm countries. There the sun shone much more brilliantly than Thumbelina had ever known it. The sky seemed twice as high, and along the roadside hedges grew the most delicious green and purple grapes; lemons and oranges hung from trees; the air was fragrant with myrtle and many sweet herbs; and about the paths ran many lovely children playing among the brightly coloured butterflies. But the swallow flew further and further still, where the scene grew more and more beautiful. And there, under great green trees, by a lake of sapphire blue, stood a palace, built long ago of dazzling white marble, with vines growing round its tall pillars. Right on top of the pillars were many swallows' nests, and in one of them lived Thumbelina's bird.

'Here is my home,' he said. 'But if you like to choose for yourself one of these beautiful flowers growing just below, I will set you down on it, and you shall live there as happily as you could wish.'

'Ah, how I should love that!' she cried, clapping her little hands.

A great white column lay fallen on the ground. It was broken into three pieces, and between them grew beautiful tall white flowers. The swallow flew down with Thumbelina and set her on one of the petals. And what a surprise she had! There, in the middle of the flower, was a little prince, as fine and delicate as if he were made of glass. He had the prettiest gold crown upon his head, and bright and shining wings upon his shoulders, and he was no bigger than Thumbelina herself. He was the guardian-spirit of the flower. In every flower was a little creature just like himself, but this one was king of them all.

'How beautiful he is!' whispered Thumbelina to the swallow. The little prince was at first quite alarmed at the bird, which seemed to him quite a giant; but when he beheld Thumbelina he was filled with joy; he thought her the loveliest girl he had ever seen, even among his flower fairies. He took his golden crown from his head and laid it on hers, and asked what her name was, and if she would consent to be his wife, and be queen of all the flowers.

Well, this was a husband she could truly love – very different from the toad's son or the old mole with his velvet coat. And so she said yes to the handsome prince. Then, from every flower rose a tiny creature, girl or boy, man or lady, so small and so beautiful that it was thrilling to see them. Each one brought Thumbelina a present, but best of all was a pair of beautiful wings. They were fastened to Thumbelina's shoulders, and now she too could fly from flower to flower. Everyone rejoiced; it was like a wonderful summer party. The swallow in his nest above joined in and sang for them the finest song he knew. But he was sad at heart, for he was so fond of Thumbelina that he never wished to be parted from her.

'You shall not be called Thumbelina any more,' said the flower-prince. 'It's not pretty enough for one as beautiful as you. We shall call you Maia.'

'Good-bye, good-bye,' said the swallow, when it was time for him to fly away from the warm countries to Denmark once again. There he had a little nest by the window of the man who tells fairy tales. 'Listen, listen,' the swallow trilled to the fairy tale teller – and that is how we come to know this story.

The Emperor's New Clothes

Many years ago there lived an Emperor. He was so passionately fond of fine new clothes that he spent all his money and time on dressing up. He cared nothing for his army, nor for going to the theatre, nor for driving out in his carriage among the people – except as a chance for showing off his latest outfit. He had a different coat for every hour of the day; and at times when you'd be told of other monarchs, 'He's holding a council,' in *his* case the answer would be, 'The Emperor is in his dressing-room.'

Life was cheerful enough in the city where he lived. Strangers were always arriving, and one day a pair of shady characters turned up; they claimed to be weavers. But the cloth they wove (so they said) wasn't only exceptionally beautiful but had magical properties; even when made into clothes it was invisible to anyone who was either unfit for his job or particularly stupid. 'Excellent!' thought the Emperor. 'What a chance to discover which men in my kingdom aren't fit for the posts they hold – and which are the wise ones and the fools. Yes! that stuff must be woven and made into clothes at once!' And he gave the two rogues a large sum of money so that they could start.

So the rascally pair set up two looms and behaved as if they were working hard; but actually there was nothing on the machines at all. Before long they were demanding the finest silk and golden thread; these they crammed into their own pockets, and went on moving their arms at the empty looms until far into the night.

After a time, the Emperor thought, 'I really *would* like to know how they are getting on.' But when he recalled that no one who was stupid, or unfit for his work, could see the cloth, he felt rather awkward about going himself. It was not that he had any doubts about his own abilities, of course – yet he felt that it might be best to send someone else for a start. After all, everyone in the city knew the special powers of the cloth; everyone was longing to find out how foolish or incompetent his neighbours were.

'I know, I'll send my honest old minister to the weavers,' he decided. 'He's the right man, as sensible as can be; and one can complain about the way he does his job.'

So the good old minister went into the room where the two rogues were pretending to work at the looms. 'Heaven help us!' he thought, and his eyes opened wider and wider. 'I can't see anything.' But he kept his thoughts to himself.

The two swindlers begged him to step closer; did he not agree that the patterns were beautiful?

the colours delightful? And they waved their hands at the empty looms. But though the poor old minister peered and stared, he still could see nothing, for the simple reason that nothing was there to see.

'Heavens!' he thought. 'Am I really stupid after all? That has never occurred to me – and it had better not occur to anyone else! Am I really unfit for my office? No – it will never do to say that I can't see any cloth.'

'Well, don't you admire it?' said one of the false weavers, still moving his hands. 'You haven't said a word!'

'Oh – it's charming, quite delightful,' said the poor old minister, peering through his spectacles. 'The pattern – the colours – yes, I must tell the Emperor that I find them truly remarkable.'

'Well, that's very encouraging,' said the two weavers, and they pointed out the details of the pattern and the different colours worked into it. The old minister listened carefully so that he could repeat it all to the Emperor. And this he did.

The two impostors now asked for a further supply of money, silk and golden thread; they had to have it, they said, to finish the cloth. But everything that they were given went straight into their own pockets; not a stitch appeared on the looms. Yet they went on busily moving their hands at the empty machines.

Presently the Emperor sent another honest official to see how the weaving was going on, and if the stuff would soon be ready. The same thing happened to him as to the minister; he looked and looked, but as there was nothing there but the empty looms, nothing was all he saw.

'Isn't it lovely material?' said the cheats. And they held out the imaginary stuff before him, pointing out the pattern which didn't exist.

'I don't believe that I'm stupid,' thought the official. 'I suppose I'm really not the right man for my job. Well, I should never have thought it! And nobody else had better think it, either.' So he made admiring noises about the cloth he could not see, and told the men that he was particularly pleased with the colours and design. 'Yes,' he reported to the Emperor, 'it's magnificent.'

The news of the remarkable stuff was soon all round the town. And now the Emperor made up his mind to see it while it was still on the looms. So, with a number of carefully chosen attendants – among them the two honest officials who had already been there – he went to the weaving room, where the rogues were performing their antics as busily as ever.

'What splendid cloth!' said the old minister. 'Observe the design, Your Majesty! Observe the colours!' said the worthy official. And they pointed to the empty looms, for they were sure that everyone else could see the material.

'This is terrible!' thought the Emperor. 'I can't see a thing! Am I stupid? Am I unfit to be Emperor? That is too frightful to think of.' 'Oh, it is charming, charming,' he said aloud. 'It has our highest approval.' He nodded in a satisfied way towards the empty looms; on no account must he admit that he saw nothing there at all.

And the courtiers with him stared there too, each one with secret alarm at seeing not a single thread. But aloud they echoed the Emperor's words: 'Charming, charming!' And they advised him to use the splendid cloth for the new set of royal robes he would wear for a great procession taking place in the near future. 'It is magnificent, so unusual . . .' Yes, you could hear such words all around. And the Emperor gave each of the impostors a knightly decoration to hang in his buttonhole, and the title of Imperial Court Official of the Loom.

All through the night before the procession day, the rogues pretended to work, with sixteen candles around them. Everyone could see how busy they were, trying to get the Emperor's outfit finished in time. They pretended to take the stuff from the looms; they cut away in the air with big tailor's scissors; they stitched and stitched with needles that had no thread; and at last they announced: 'The clothes are ready!'

The Emperor came with his noblest courtiers to look, and the two impostors held up their arms as if lifting something. 'Here are the trousers,' they said. 'Here is the jacket, here is the cloak' – and so on. 'They are as light as gossamer; you would think, from the feel, that you had nothing on at all – but that, of course, is the beauty of it.'

'Yes, indeed,' said all the attendants; but they could not see anything, for there was nothing there to see.

'If Your Imperial Majesty will graciously take off the clothes you are wearing, we shall have the honour of putting on the new ones here in front of the great mirror.'

The Emperor took off his clothes, and the rogues pretended to hand him the new set, one item at a time. They then put their arms around his waist, and appeared to be fastening his train, the final touch.

The Emperor turned about and twisted before the glass.

'How elegant it looks! What a perfect fit!' the courtiers murmured. 'What rich material! What splendid colours! Have you ever seen such magnificence?'

'Your Majesty,' said the Chief Master of Ceremonies, 'the canopy waits outside.' The canopy was to be borne over his head in the procession.

'Well,' said the Emperor, 'I am ready. It really is an excellent fit, don't you think?' And he turned himself round again once more in front of the mirror, as if taking a final look. The courtiers who were to carry the train stooped, as if to lift something from the floor, then raised their hands before

them. They were not going to let people think that they saw nothing there.

So the Emperor walked in stately procession under the splendid canopy; and everyone in the streets or at the windows exclaimed, 'Doesn't the Emperor look magnificent! Those new clothes – aren't they marvellous! Just look at the train! The elegance of it!'

For nobody dared to admit that he couldn't see any clothes; this would have meant that he was a fool or no good at his job. None of the Emperor's gorgeous outfits had ever been so much admired.

Then a child's puzzled voice was clearly heard. 'He's got nothing on!' 'These innocents! What ridiculous things they say!' said the child's father. But the whisper passed through the crowd: 'That child there says that the Emperor has nothing on; the Emperor has nothing on!'

And presently, everyone there was repeating, 'He's got nothing on!' At last, it seemed to the Emperor too that they must be right. But he thought to himself, 'I must not stop or it will spoil the procession.' So he marched on even more proudly than before, and the courtiers continued to carry a train that was not there at all.

The Little Mermaid

Far, far out to sea the water is as blue as the petals of the loveliest cornflower, and as clear as the clearest glass; but it is deep, very deep, deeper than any anchor has ever sunk. Countless church towers would have to be placed one on top of one

another to reach from the sea-bed to the surface. Down in those depths live the mer-people.

Now you must not think for a moment that there is nothing down below but bare white sand. No, indeed – the most wonderful trees and plants grow there, with stems and leaves so lithe and sensitive that they wave and sway with the slightest stir of the water; they might be living creatures. All kinds of fish, both large and small, glide in and out of the branches, just like birds in the air up here. In the very deepest part of all is the Mer-King's palace. Its walls are of coral, and the long pointed windows are of the clearest amber, while the roof is made of cockleshells, which open and close with the waves. That's a splendid sight, for each holds a shining pearl; any single one would be the pride of a queen's crown.

The Mer-King here had been a widower for many years; his dowager mother kept house for him. She was a wise old lady, though rather too proud of her royal rank; that's why she always wore twelve oysters on her tail while other high-born mer-folk were allowed no more than six. But she deserved special praise for the care she took of the little mer-princesses, her granddaughters.

There were six of them, all beautiful, but the youngest was the most beautiful of all. Her skin was like a rose petal, pure and clear; her eyes were as blue as the deepest lake. But, like the others, she had no feet; her body ended in a fish's tail. All day long she and her sisters would play down there in the palace, in and out of the vast rooms where living sea-flowers grew from the walls. When the great amber windows were open the fish would swim inside and let themselves be stroked.

Outside the palace was a large garden with flame-red and sea-blue trees. The fruit all shone like gold, and the flowers looked like glowing fire among the moving stems and leaves. The ground itself was of the finest sand, but blue as a sulphur flame. A strange blue-violet light lay over everything; you might have thought that, instead of being far down under the sea, you were high up in the air, with nothing over and under you but sky. On days of perfect calm you could see the sun; it looked like a crimson flower, with rays of light streaming out of its centre.

Each of the little princesses had her own small plot in the garden, where she could dig and plant whatever she wished. One made her flower-bed in the shape of a whale; another made hers like a mermaid. But the youngest had hers perfectly round, like the sun, and the only flowers she planted there were like smaller suns in their glow and colour.

She was a strange child, quiet and thoughtful. While the other sisters decorated their gardens with wonderful things from the wrecks of ships, the only ornament she would have was a beautiful marble carving, a lovely boy made out of pure white stone. This too had sunk to the sea-bed from a wreck. Beside this marble boy she planted a rose-red tree like a weeping willow; it grew apace, its branches bending over the stone figure until they touched the deep-blue sand below.

Nothing pleased the youngest princess more than to hear about the far-off world of humans. She made the old grandmother tell her all she knew about ships and towns, people and animals. It was a strange and wonderful thought to her that the flowers on earth had a sweet smell, for they had none at all in the sea.

'As soon as you are fifteen,' the grandmother told her granddaughters, 'you may rise to the surface, and sit on the rocks in the moonlight and watch the great ships sail by. If you have enough courage you may even see woods and towns!' The following year the oldest of the sisters would be fifteen; but as for the others – well, each was a year younger than the next, so the youngest of them all still had five years to wait. But each promised to tell the rest what she had seen, and what she had found most surprising in the human world above. Their grandmother never told them enough, and there was so much they wanted to know.

But none of the six had a greater wish to learn about the mysterious earth above than the youngest (the very one who had the longest time to wait), the one who was so thoughtful and quiet. Many a night she would stand at the open window and gaze up through the dark-blue water where the fishes frisked with waving fins and tails. She could see the moon and stars; their light was rather pale, to be sure, but seen through the water they looked much larger than they do to us. If ever a kind of dark cloud glided along beneath them, she knew that it was either a whale swimming over her, or a ship full of human people. Those humans never imagined that a beautiful little mermaid was below, stretching up her white hands towards the keel.

And now came the time when the eldest princess was fifteen, and was allowed to rise to the surface. As soon as she was home again she had a hundred things to tell the others. But what did she like best of all? Lying on a sandbank in the moonlight when the sea was calm, she told them, gazing at the big city, near to the coast, where the lights were twinkling like a hundred stars, listening to the busy noise and stir of traffic and people, seeing all the towers and spires of the churches, hearing the ringing of the bells. And just because she couldn't go to the city, she longed to do this more than anything.

Oh, how intently the youngest sister listened! And later in the evening, when she stood at the open window and gazed up through the dark-blue water, she thought of the great city, and then she seemed to hear the ring of church bells echoing all the way down to her.

The next year the second sister was allowed to rise up through the water and swim wherever she wished. She reached the surface just as the sun was going down, and that was the sight that she thought loveliest of all. The whole sky was a blaze of gold, she said; as for the clouds – well, she couldn't find words to describe how beautiful they were, crimson and violet, sailing high overhead. But moving much more swiftly, a flock of wild swans like a long white ribbon had flown across the waves towards the setting sun. She too had swum towards the sun, but it sank in the water, and the brightness vanished from sea and sky.

The year after that, the third sister had her chance. She was the most adventurous of the lot, and swam up a wide river that flowed into the sea. She saw green hills planted with grape-vines; she had glimpses of farms and castles through the trees of the great forests. She heard the singing of birds; she felt the warmth of the sun – indeed, it was so hot that she often had to dive down to cool her burning face. In the curve of a little bay a group of human children were splashing about in the water, quite naked; she wanted to play with them, but they scampered off in a fright.

The fourth sister was not so bold. She kept to mid-ocean, well away from the shore, and that, she declared, gave the best view of all; you could see for miles around. She had seen ships, but so far away that they looked like seagulls. The friendly dolphins had turned somersaults; great whales had spouted jets of water – it was like being surrounded by a hundred waterfalls.

Then came the turn of the fifth sister. Her birthday happened to fall in winter, and so she saw what the others had not seen on their first view of the world above. The sea looked quite green; great icebergs floated about, each one as beautiful as a pearl, she said – yet vaster than the church towers built by men. They appeared in the strangest shapes, glittering like diamonds. She had seated herself on one of the largest, and the sailors in passing ships were filled with terror, and steered in wide curves as far away as they could get from the iceberg where she sat, her long hair streaming in the wind. Late that evening the sky had become heavy and overcast; lightning flashed; thunder rolled and rumbled, and the dark waves lifted huge blocks of ice high into the air. Sails were lowered on all the ships; humans aboard were struck with fear and dread; but the mermaid still sat peacefully on her floating iceberg, and calmly watched the violet flashes of lightning zigzagging down into the glittering sea.

The first time each of the sisters rose above the surface she was enchanted by all the new and wonderful sights; but now that the five were old enough to journey up whenever they liked, they soon lost interest; after a short time at the surface they longed to be home again. The most beautiful place in the world was deep beneath the sea.

Still, there were many evenings when the five sisters would link arms and rise to the surface together. They had lovely voices – no human voice was ever so hauntingly beautiful – and when a storm blew up, and they thought that a ship might be wrecked, they would swim in front of the vessel and sing about the delights of their world beneath the sea; the sailors should have no fear of coming there. But the sailors never understood the songs; they fancied they were hearing the sound of the storm. Nor could they ever see for themselves the paradise down below, for when the ship sank, they were drowned, and only drowned men ever reached the Mer-King's palace.

On those evenings, the youngest was left behind all alone, gazing after them. She would have cried, but a mermaid has no tears, and that makes her feel more grief than if she had.

And then at last she was fifteen.

'There now! We're getting you off our hands at last!' said her grandmother, the old queen Mother. 'Come along, and let me dress you up like your sisters.' And she put a wreath of white lilies on her head, but every petal was really half a pearl. 'Good-bye,' the little mermaid said, and floated up through the water as lightly as a bubble.

The sun had just set when her head touched the surface, but the clouds still had a gleam of gold and rose. Up in the pale pink sky the evening star shone out, clear and radiant; the air was soft and mild, and the sea was calm as glass. A great three-masted ship was lying there; only one sail was set, because there wasn't a breath of wind, and the sailors were idly waiting in the rigging and yard-arms. There were sounds of music and singing, and as the night grew darker hundreds of coloured lanterns lit the scene; it looked as if flags of all the nations were flying in the wind.

The little mermaid swam right up to a porthole. Every time she rose with the lift of the waves she could see through the clear glass a crowd of people in splendid clothes – and the handsomest of all was a young prince with large dark eyes. He could not have been much older than sixteen – in fact, this was his birthday, and the cause of all the excitement. Now sailors began to dance on the decks, and when the young prince stepped out among them, over a hundred rockets shot up in the air. They made the night as bright as day, so that the little mermaid was quite terrified, and dived down under the water. But she soon popped up her head again, and then she thought that all the stars of heaven were falling down towards her. She had never seen fireworks. Catherine-wheels were spinning round like suns; rockets like fiery fishes soared into the sky, and all this was reflected in the sea. On the ship itself there was so much light that you could make out the smallest rope, and the features of every face. Oh, how handsome the young prince was! There he stood, shaking hands with one guest after another, laughing and smiling, while the music rang out into the night.

It was growing late, but the little mermaid could not take her eyes from the ship and the

handsome prince. The coloured lamps were put out; no more rockets flew up; no more guns were fired. Yet deep down in the sea there was a murmuring and a rumbling. The waves rose higher; great clouds massed together; lightning flashed in the distance – a terrible storm was on the way. And so the crew took in sail as the great ship tossed about. The waves rose like huge black mountains, higher than the masts themselves; but the ship dived down like a swan between the billows and then rode up again on the towering crests. To the little mermaid all this was delightful – but it was no joke to the sailors. The vessel creaked and cracked; its thick planks bent under the pounding blows of the waves, the mast snapped in the middle – and then the ship heeled over on its side, and water came rushing into the hold. Now at last the little mermaid realized that they were in danger; even she herself had to look out for the broken beams and planks that were churning about in the water. At one moment it was so pitch black that she could see nothing at all; then, when lightning flashed, it was so bright that she could distinguish every one on board. They all seemed desperately trying to save their own lives; but she looked about only for one, the young prince. And just as the ship broke up she saw him, sinking down, drawn below into the deep heart of the sea.

For a moment she felt nothing but joy, for he would be coming into her own country; but then she remembered that humans could not live in the water, and that only as a drowned man could he ever enter her father's palace. No, he must not die! So she swam out through the drifting, jostling beams; they might have crushed her, but the thought never entered her head. Then, diving deep into the water, and rising up high with the waves, she at last reached the young prince, who could scarcely keep afloat any longer in the raging sea. His arms and legs were almost too weak to move; his beautiful eyes were closed, and he would certainly have drowned if the little mermaid had not come. She held his head above the water and let the waves carry the two of them where they would.

When morning came, the storm was over, but not a trace of the ship was to be seen. The sun rose, flame-red and brilliant, out of the water, and seemed to bring a tinge of life to the pale face of the prince; but his eyes remained shut. The mermaid kissed his forehead and stroked back his wet hair. The thought came to her that he was very much like the marble statue in her own little garden; she kissed him again. Oh, if only he would live!

And now she saw dry land in front of her, and high blue mountains whose tops were white with snow. Not far from the shore were lovely green woods, and before them stood a church, or abbey – she did not know what to call it, but a building of that kind. Orange and lemon trees grew in its garden, and tall palms by the gate. Near by, the sea formed a little bay, very calm and still, but deep, with cliffs all round where fine white sand had piled. She swam to this bay with the handsome prince, and laid him on the sand, in the warmth of the sun, taking care that his head lay well away from the sea.

Now the bells rang out in the great white building. So the little mermaid swam further out and hid behind some rocks rising out of the water, covering herself in sea foam so that no one would notice her. From there she watched to see who would come to rescue the poor prince lying in the sand. Quite soon a young girl appeared. The sight of the half-drowned figure seemed to frighten her, but only for a moment. Then she went and fetched other people, and the mermaid saw the prince revive and smile at everybody around him. But he did not turn and smile at her, for of course, he had no idea that she was the one who saved him. She felt terribly sad, and after he had been taken into the building she dived down sorrowfully into the water and returned to her father's palace.

She had always been quiet and thoughtful, but now she became much more so. Her sisters asked what she had seen on her first journey into the human world, but she told them nothing.

On many evenings, and many mornings, she glided up to the place where she had left the prince. She saw the fruit grow ripe in the garden, and she saw it gathered in; she saw the snow melt on the high mountains – but she never saw the prince. Her one comfort was to sit in her little garden clasping her arms round the beautiful marble statue which was so much like the prince. But she no longer tended her flowers; they grew like wild things, trailing over the paths, weaving their long stems and leaves in and out of the boughs of the trees until the whole place was in shadow.

At last she could bear it no longer, and told the story to one of her sisters; very soon the others knew it too – nobody else, of course, except one or two other mermaids who told only their best friends. One of these was able to tell her who the young prince was; and where his kingdom lay.

'Come, little sister,' said the other princesses. And then, with their arms over one another's shoulders, they rose to the surface and floated in a long row just in front of the prince's palace. It was built of a shining gold-coloured stone with great marble steps, some leading right down into the sea. Towering above the roof were magnificent golden domes, and between the pillars surrounding the building stood marble statues; they almost seemed alive. Through the glass of the tall windows you could see into splendid halls, hung with priceless silken curtains and tapestries. In the centre of the largest hall a great fountain was playing, the water leaping as high as the glass dome in the roof. The sun's rays shone through the dome, lighting the fountain and the lovely plants that grew in the great pool below.

Now that the little mermaid knew where he lived, she would rise to the surface and watch there, night after night. She would swim much closer to land than any of the others had ever dared; she even went right up the narrow canal under the marble balcony, which cast its long shadow over the water. There she would sit and gaze at the young prince, who believed that he was quite alone in the moonlight.

Often in the evenings she would see him setting out in his splendid boat with its flying flags, while music played. She would peep out from between the green rushes, and people who saw a silvery flash thought only that it was a swan spreading its wings. Many a time, later in the night, when the fishermen waited out at sea with their fiery torches, she heard them saying so much that was good about the young prince; this always made her glad that she had saved his life when he lay almost dead on the waves. But he knew nothing at all about that.

She felt closer and closer to human people, and longed more and more to go up and join them. There was so much that she wished to know, but her sisters could not answer her questions. So she asked her old grandmother; *she* knew quite a few things about the upper world, as she very properly called the lands above the sea.

'If humans are not drowned, can they live for

ever?' asked the little mermaid. 'Do they never die, as we do here in the sea?'

'Yes indeed,' said the old lady, 'they too have to die; and their lives are even shorter than ours. We can live for three hundred years, but when our time comes to an end we are only foam on the water; we are like the green rushes. But humans have a soul which lives on after the body has turned to dust. It flies up through the sky to the shining stars. Just as we rise out of the sea and gaze at the human world, they rise up to unknown places which we shall never reach.'

'Why, I would give all my hundreds of years in exchange for being a human, even for just one day, if I then had the chance of a place in the heavenly world,' said the little mermaid, very sadly.

'You mustn't think such things!' said the old lady. 'We are much happier here, and much better off too than the folk up there.'

'But is there nothing I can do to get an immortal soul?' asked the little mermaid.

'No,' said the old lady. 'Only if a human being loved you so dearly that you were more to him than father or mother; only if he clung to you with all his heart and soul, letting the priest place his right hand in yours, promising to be true to you, here and in all eternity – then you too would share the human destiny. But that can never happen. The very thing that is so beautiful here in the sea – I mean your mermaid's tail – they think quite ugly up there on earth. Their taste is so peculiar that they have to have two clumsy props called legs if they want to look elegant.'

That made the little mermaid sigh, and look sadly at her fish's tail.

'Let us be cheerful,' said the old lady. 'Let us make the best of the three hundred years of our life by leaping and dancing; it's a good long time after all. Then when it's over we can have our fill of sleep; it will be all the more welcome and agreeable. Tonight, we'll have a court ball.'

This was something far more splendid than any we see on earth. The walls and ceilings of the great ballroom were of crystal glass, thick, but perfectly clear. Several hundred enormous shells, rose-red and emerald-green, were set in rows on either side, each holding a bluish flame; these lit up the whole room and shone out through the walls, giving a sapphire glow to the sea outside. Countless fishes, large and small, could be seen swimming towards the glass, some with scales of glowing violet, others silver and gold.

Through the middle of the ballroom flowed a broad swift stream, and on it mermen and mermaids danced to a marvellous sound – the sound of their own singing. No humans have such beautiful voices – and the sweetest singer of all was the little mermaid. When she sang, the whole assembly clapped their hands; for a moment she felt a thrill of joy, for she knew that she had the most beautiful voice of all who live on earth or in the sea. But she could not forget the handsome prince; and could not forget that she had no immortal soul. And so she slipped out of her father's palace, and sat in her little garden, thinking her sad thoughts.

Suddenly, echoing down through the water, she heard the sound of horn-music. 'Ah, he must be sailing up there,' she mused, 'the one whom I love more than father and mother, the one who is never out of my thoughts. To win his love and to gain an immortal soul, I would dare anything! Yes – while my sisters are dancing in our father's palace I will call on the old sea witch. I have always been dreadfully afraid of her, but she may be able to tell me what to do.'

And so the little mermaid left her garden and set off for the roaring whirlpools, for the old enchantress lived just beyond. She had never taken that grim path before. No flowers grew there, no sea grass even. All she could see was bare grey sand stretching away from the whirlpool, where the water went swirling round as if huge and crazy millwheels were turning all the time, dragging everything caught in them down, down into unknown depths. To reach the sea witch's domain she had to go right through these raging waters, and after that there was no other way but over a long swampy stretch of bubbling mud; the witch called it her peat-bog. Behind this lay her house, deep in an eerie forest. The trees and bushes were of the polyp kind, half creature and half plant; they looked like hundred-headed snakes growing out of the earth. The branches were really long slimy arms with fingers like writhing worms; from joint to joint they never stopped moving, and everything they could touch they twined around and held in a lasting grip.

The little mermaid was terrified as she stood on the edge of this frightful forest. She almost turned back – but then she thought of the prince and the human soul, and plucked up courage. She tied her long flowing hair tightly round her head to keep it from the clutch of the polyp-fingers; then, folding her hands together, she darted along as a fish darts through the water, in and out of the hideous branches, which reached out their waving arms and fingers after her.

Now she came to a large slimy open space in the dreadful forest, where fat water-snakes were frisking about, showing their ugly yellow-white undersides; the sea witch called these her little pets. In the very middle a house had been built from the bones of shipwrecked humans, and here sat the witch herself.

'I know well enough why you are here,' said the witch. 'It's a foolish notion! However, you shall have your way, for it will bring you nothing but trouble, my pretty princess! You want to get rid of your fish's tail and have two stumps instead, like human beings; then, you hope, the young prince will fall in love with you, and you'll be able to marry him, and get an immortal soul into the bargain.' With that, the witch uttered such a loud and horrible laugh that the creatures coiling over her fell sprawling to the ground.

'You've come just in the nick of time,' said the witch. 'Tomorrow, after sunrise, I wouldn't be able to help for another year. Now I shall make a special potion for you; before the sun rises you must swim with it to the land, sit down and drink it up. Then your tail will divide in two and shrink into what those humans call a lovely pair of legs. But it'll hurt; it will be like a sharp sword going through you. Everyone will say that you are the loveliest child they have ever seen. You will glide along – ah, more gracefully than any dancer, but every step you take will be like treading on a sharp knife. If you are willing to suffer all this, then I will help you.'

'Yes, I am willing,' said the little mermaid. Her voice trembled, but she fixed her thoughts on the prince, and the chance to gain an immortal soul.

'But remember,' said the witch, 'when once you've taken a human shape, you can never again be a mermaid. You can never go down through the water to your sisters, or to your father's palace! And if you fail to win the prince's love, so that he forgets both father and mother for your sake, and lets the priest join you together as man and wife, you won't get that immortal soul. On the first morning after he marries another, your heart will break, and you will turn into foam on the water.'

'I am willing,' said the little mermaid. She was now as pale as death.

'But I want my payment too,' said the witch, 'and it's not a small one either. You have the most exquisite voice of anyone here in the sea. You think that you'll be able to charm him with it, but you're going to give that voice to me. The price of my precious drink is the finest thing you possess. For I shall have to put some of my own blood into it, to make it as sharp as a two-edged sword.'

'But if you take my voice,' said the little mermaid, 'what shall I have left?'

'Your beauty,' said the witch, 'your grace in moving, your lovely, speaking eyes – with these you can easily catch a human heart. Well, have you lost your courage? Put out your little tongue; I'll cut it off as my payment, and you shall have the magic drink.'

'Well, if it must be so,' said the little mermaid, and the witch put her cauldron on the fire to prepare the potion. 'Cleanliness is a good thing,' she remarked, and she wiped out the cauldron with a knotted bunch of snakes. Then she scratched her breast and let some black blood drip down into the pot. The steam rose up in the weirdest shapes, enough to fill anyone with fear and dread. Every moment the witch cast some different item into the cauldron, and when it was really boiling it sounded like the weeping of a crocodile. At last the brew was ready – and it looked like the clearest water.

'There you are!' said the witch, and she cut off the little mermaid's tongue. Now she had no voice; she could neither sing nor speak.

'If those polyps catch hold of you when you are going back through the wood,' said the witch, 'just throw a drop of the potion on them. You'll see!' But the little mermaid had no need to do that, for the polyps drew back in fear when they saw the potion glittering in her hand like a star. So she came back without delay through the swamp, the forest, and the roaring whirlpool.

She could see her father's palace; the lights were out in the great ballroom – no doubt they were all asleep by now. Yet she dared not go and look, for she was dumb, and she was about to leave them for ever. She felt as if her heart would break with grief. She crept into the garden, took one flower from the flower-bed of each sister, threw a thousand kisses towards the palace, and rose up through the dark-blue sea.

The sun had not yet risen when she came in sight of the prince's palace and made her way up the splendid marble steps. The moon was shining bright and clear. The little mermaid drank the burning drink. A two-edged sword seemed to thrust itself through her delicate body; she fainted, and lay as though dead.

When the sun rose, shining across the sea, she woke, and the sharp pain returned, but there in front of her stood the young prince. His jet-black eyes were fixed on her so intently that she cast her own eyes down – and then she saw that the fish's tail was gone, and that she had instead the prettiest neat white legs that any girl could wish for. But she had no clothes, and so she wrapped herself in her long flowing hair. The prince asked who she was, and how she had come there, but she could only gaze back at him sweetly and sadly with her deep blue eyes, for of course she could not speak. Then he took her by the hand and led her into the palace. Every step she took made her feel as if she were treading on pointed swords, just as the witch had warned her – yet she endured it gladly. Holding the prince's hand, she trod the ground, light as air, and the prince and all who saw her marvelled at her graceful, gliding walk.

She was given rich dresses of finest silk and muslin. All agreed that she was the loveliest maiden in the palace. But she was dumb; she could neither sing nor speak. Beautiful slave girls in silk and gold came forward to sing for the prince and his royal parents. One of them sang more movingly than the rest, and the prince clapped his hands and smiled at her. This saddened the little mermaid, for she knew that her own lost voice was far more beautiful. She thought: 'If only he could know that I gave away my voice for ever, just to be near him.'

Next, the slave girls danced in graceful gliding motion to thrilling music, and then the little mermaid rose on to the tips of her toes, and floated across the floor, dancing as no one had ever yet danced. With every movement she seemed lovelier, and her eyes spoke more deeply to the heart than all the slave girls' singing.

The whole court was delighted, and the prince most of all; he called her his little foundling. So she went on dancing, though every time her foot touched the ground she seemed to be treading on sharp knives. The prince declared that she must never leave him, and she was given a place to sleep outside his door on a velvet cushion.

He had a boy's suit made for her so that she could go riding with him on horseback. They rode through the sweet-smelling woods, where the green boughs touched her shoulders, and the little birds twittered away in the fresh green leaves. She joined the prince when he climbed high mountains, and though her delicate feet were cut so that all could see, she only laughed, and kept at his side until they could see the clouds sailing beneath them like a flock of birds on the way to distant lands.

At night in the prince's palace, when the others were all asleep, she would go out to the wide marble steps and cool her burning feet in the cold sea water; and then she would think of those down below in the depths of the waves.

One night, her sisters rose to the surface, arm in arm, singing most mournfully as they swam across the water; she waved to them and they recognized her, and told her how unhappy she had made them all. After that, they used to visit her every night; once, in the far distance, she perceived her old grandmother, who hadn't been to the surface for years, together with the Merman-King himself, wearing his crown. They both stretched out their hands towards her, but they would not venture as near to land as her sisters.

As each day passed, the prince grew fonder and fonder of her. He loved her as one loves a dear good child; but the idea of making her his queen never entered his head. And yet, if she did not become his wife she would never gain an immortal soul, and on his wedding morning to another she would dissolve into foam on the sea.

'Do you not love me more than all the rest?' the little mermaid's eyes seemed to say when he took her in his arms and kissed her delicate forehead. 'Yes, of course, you are dearest of all to me,' said the prince, 'because you have the truest heart of all. Besides, you also remind me of a young girl I once saw, and doubt if I shall ever see again. I was on a ship that was wrecked, and the waves drove me to land near a sacred temple, which was tended by many young maidens. The youngest of them found me on the beach and saved my life. I saw her twice, no more, but she was the only one I could ever love in this world, and you are so like her that you almost take her place in my heart. But she belongs to the holy temple, so it is my good fortune that you have been sent to me. We shall never part.'

'Ah, he doesn't know that I was the one who saved his life,' thought the little mermaid. 'He doesn't know that I carried him through the waves to the temple in the wood, that I waited in the foam to see if anyone would come to rescue him, and that I saw the beautiful maiden whom he loves more than me.' The mermaid sighed deeply – weep she could not. 'The maiden belongs to the holy temple' – those were his words. 'She will never come out into the world, so they will not meet again. I am here; I am with him; I see him every day. I will care for him, love him, give up my life for him!'

But now the rumour rose that the prince was to be married, to the lovely daughter of the neighbouring king, and because of this he was fitting out a splendid ship. 'The prince is supposed to be travelling forth to visit the next door kingdom,' people said. 'But it's really to call on the king's daughter.' The little mermaid shook her head and laughed; she knew the prince's mind better than anyone. 'I am obliged to make this journey,' he had said to her. 'I have to meet the charming princess – my mother and father insist on that – but they cannot force me to bring her home as my bride. I cannot love this stranger! She will not remind me of the fair maid of the temple, as you do. If I have to find a bride, my choice would be you, my dear dumb foundling with the speaking eyes.' And he kissed her rose-red mouth.

'You have no fear of the sea, my silent child!'

he said, as they stood on the splendid ship that was to carry him to the lands of the neighbouring king. And he told her of storms and calm, of strange fish in the deep, and the marvels that divers had seen down there; she smiled at his accounts, for of course she knew more about the world beneath the waves than anyone.

In the moonlit night, when everyone but the helmsman at the wheel was asleep, she sat by the ship's rail, gazing into the calm water. She thought that she could make out her father's palace, with her old grandmother standing on the highest tower, in her silver crown, peering up through the racing tides at the vessel overhead. Then her sisters came to the surface and looked at her with eyes full of sorrow, wringing their white hands. She waved to them and smiled, and wanted to tell them that all was going well and happily with her; but then one of the cabin boys drew near, and her sisters sank below.

Next morning the ship sailed into the harbour of the neighbouring king's fine city. All the church bells were ringing; trumpets blared from the tall towers, while soldiers stood on parade with flying flags and glinting bayonets. Every day was like a fête; no sooner was one ball or party over than another began – but the princess was not there. She was being brought up in a holy temple, they said, where she was learning the ways of wisdom that her royal role would need. At last, however, she arrived.

The little mermaid waited by, eager to see her beauty, and she had to admit that it would be hard to find a lovelier human girl. Her skin was so delicate and pure, and behind her long lashes smiled a pair of steadfast dark-blue eyes.

'It is you!' said the prince. 'You were the one who saved me when I lay almost dead on the shore!' And he held the blushing princess in his arms. 'Oh, I am overjoyed,' he said to the little mermaid. 'My dearest wish – more than I ever dared hope for – has come true. I know you will share in my happiness, because no one anywhere cares for me more than you.' The little mermaid kissed his head, though she felt that her heart would break. His wedding morning would bring her death, and turn her to a wisp of foam on the sea.

All the church bells rang out; heralds rode through the streets to proclaim the news. Sweet-smelling oils burned on every altar in precious silver lamps. The priests swung incense vessels; bride and bridegroom joined their hands and received the bishop's blessing. The little mermaid, in silk and gold, stood holding the bridal train, but her ears never heard the festive music, nor did her eyes see the holy ceremony. This was her last day alive in the world, and she thought of all that she had lost.

That evening the bride and bridegroom went aboard the ship. A royal tent of gold and purple had been set up on the main deck with silken cushions and hangings, and there the bridal pair were to sleep in that calm cool pleasant night.

The sails filled out in the breeze, and the vessel flew swiftly and lightly over the shining sea.

As darkness fell, lanterns of every colour were lit, and on the deck the sailors danced merrily. The little mermaid remembered the first time she had come to the surface, and had gazed on just such a joyful scene. And now she too was joining in the dance, lightly gliding and swerving as a swallow does to avoid a pursuer. She could hear the admiring voices and applause, for never before had she danced so brilliantly. Sharp knives seemed to cut her delicate feet, yet she hardly felt them, so deep was the pain in her heart. She could not forget that this was the last night she would ever see the one for whom she had left her home and family, had given up her beautiful voice, and had day by day endured unending torment, of which he knew nothing at all. An eternal night awaited her.

At last, well after midnight, the merrymaking drew to a close. The prince kissed his lovely bride, and they went to the royal tent.

The ship grew hushed and silent; only the helmsman was still awake at the wheel. The little mermaid leaned her white arms on the rail and looked eastwards for a sign of the dawn; the first ray of the sun, she knew, would mean her end. Suddenly, rising out of the sea, she saw her sisters. They were as ghastly pale as she, and their beautiful hair no longer streamed in the wind – it had been cut off.

'We gave our hair to the witch in return for help, for something that will save you from death when morning breaks. She has given us a knife. Look! See how sharp it is! Before the sun rises you must plunge it into the prince's heart; when his warm blood splashes your feet, they will grow together into a fish's tail and you will become a mermaid once again, just as you used to be. You will be able to join us in the depths below and live out all your three hundred years before you dissolve away into salt sea foam. Hurry! Either he or you must die before the first ray of sunrise! Our old grandmother is so full of grief that her white hair has fallen out just as ours fell before the witch's scissors. Kill the prince and come back to us! Hurry! Do you see that red streak in the sky? In a few minutes the sun will rise and you will be no more.' With a strange deep sigh they sank beneath the waves.

The little mermaid drew back the purple curtain from the tent door where the prince and princess slept; she looked up at the sky where the red of dawn began to glow, looked at the sharp knife, and looked again at the prince. The knife quivered in her hand – then she flung it far out into the waves; they shone red where it fell, as though drops of blood were leaping out of the water. Once more she looked at the prince, through eyes half-glazed in death; then she threw herself from the ship into the sea, where she felt her body dissolving into foam.

And now the sun rose from the ocean, and on the foam its beams lay gentle and warm. The little mermaid had no feeling of death. She saw the bright sun, and also, floating above her, hundreds of lovely transparent creatures. Through them she could see the white sails of the ship and the rose-red clouds in the sky. Their voices were like music, but of so ethereal a kind that no human ear could hear it, just as no earthly eye could perceive them. Without wings they floated through the air, borne by their own lightness. And now the little mermaid saw that she had become like them, and was rising higher and higher above the waves.

'Where am I going?' said she, and her voice, too, sounded like those of the other beings, so ethereal that no earthly music could even echo its tune.

'To join with us, spirits of the air,' they answered. 'We do not need the love of a human being to become immortal. We fly to hot countries where the stifling breath of plague carries death to humans, and we bring them cool fresh breezes; we fill the air with scent of flowers that bring relief and healing. When we have tried to do all the good we can for three hundred years, we gain an immortal soul and eternal happiness. You, too, poor little mermaid, have striven with all your heart to do good; you have suffered and endured and have raised yourself into the higher world of the spirits of the air. Now, you too can gain an immortal soul for yourself.'

The little mermaid lifted her arms towards the heavenly sun. On the ship the bustle of waking life had started again. She saw the prince with his beautiful bride; they were searching for her, gazing sorrowfully into the moving waves. She smiled at the prince, and then, with the other children of the air, she soared up on to the rose-red cloud which floated in the sky.

'In this way, when three hundred years are passed, I shall rise into the kingdom of heaven.'

'Perhaps even sooner,' one of them whispered. 'Unseen, we glide into human homes where there are children, and whenever we find a good child, one who makes its parents happy and deserves their love, God shortens our time of trial. The child never knows when we fly through the room; if its goodness makes us smile with pleasure, a year is taken from the three hundred. But if we see a naughty, evil child, then we must weep tears of sorrow, and each tear adds one day more to our time of waiting.'

The Steadfast Tin Soldier

There were once twenty-five tin soldiers, all of them brothers, for they had all been made from the same tin kitchen spoon. They shouldered arms and looked straight before them, very smart in their red and blue uniforms. 'Tin soldiers!' That was the very first thing that they heard in this world, when the lid of their box was taken off. A little boy had shouted this and clapped his hands; he had been given them as a birthday present, and now he set them out on the table. Each soldier was exactly like the next – except for one, which had only a single leg; he was the last to be moulded, and there was not quite enough tin left. Yet he stood just as well on his one leg as the others did on their two, and he is this story's hero.

On the table where they were placed there were many other toys, but the one which everyone noticed first was a paper castle. Through its little windows you could see right into the rooms. In front of it, tiny trees were arranged round a piece of mirror, which was meant to look like a lake. Swans made of wax seemed to float on its surface, and gaze at their white reflections. The whole scene was enchanting – and the prettiest thing of all was a girl who stood in the open doorway; she too was cut out of paper, but her gauzy skirt was of finest muslin; a narrow blue ribbon crossed her shoulder like a scarf, and was held by a shining sequin almost the size of her face. This charming little creature held both of her arms stretched out, for she was a dancer; indeed, one of her legs was raised so high in the air that the tin soldier could not see it at all; he thought that she had only one leg like himself.

'Now she would be just the right wife for me,' he thought. 'But she is so grand; she lives in a castle, and I have only a box – and there are five-and-twenty of us in that! There certainly isn't room for her. Still, I can try to make her acquaintance.' So he lay down full-length behind a snuff-box which was on the table; from there he could easily watch the little paper dancer, who continued to stand on one leg without losing her balance.

When evening came, all the other tin soldiers were put in their box, and the children went to bed. Now the toys began to have games of their own; they played at visiting, and schools, and battles, and going to parties. The tin soldiers rattled in their box, for they wanted to join in, but they couldn't get the lid off. The nutcrackers turned somersaults, and the slate pencil squeaked on the slate; there was such a din that the canary woke up and took part in the talk – what's more, he did it in verse. The only two who didn't move were the tin soldier and the little dancer; she continued to stand on the point of her toe, with her arms held out; he stood just as steadily on his single leg – and never once did he take his eyes from her.

Now the clock struck twelve. Crack! – the lid flew off the snuff-box and up popped a little black goblin. There was no snuff inside the box – it was a kind of trick, a jack-in-the-box.

'Tin soldier!' screeched the goblin. 'Keep your eyes to yourself!'

But the tin soldier pretended not to hear.

'All right, just you wait till tomorrow!' said the goblin.

When morning came and the children were up again, the tin soldier was placed on the window ledge. The goblin may have been responsible, or perhaps a draught blowing through – anyhow, the window suddenly swung open, and out fell the tin soldier, all the three storeys to the ground. It was a dreadful fall! His leg pointed upwards, his head was down, and he came to a halt with his bayonet stuck between the paving stones.

The servant-girl and the little boy went to search in the street, but although they were almost treading on the soldier they somehow failed to see him. If he had called out, 'Here I am!' they would have found him easily, but he didn't think it proper behaviour to cry out when he was in uniform.

Now it began to rain; the drops fell fast – it was a drenching shower. When it was over, a pair of urchins passed. 'Look!' said one of them. 'There's a tin soldier. Let's put him out to sea.'

So they made a boat out of newspaper and put the tin soldier in the middle, and set it in the fast-flowing gutter at the edge of the street. Away he sped, and the two boys ran beside him clapping their hands. Goodness, what waves there were in that gutter-stream, what rolling tides! It had been a real downpour. The paper boat tossed up and down, sometimes whirling round and round, until the soldier felt quite giddy. But he remained as steadfast as ever, not moving a muscle, still looking straight in front of him, still shouldering arms.

All at once the boat entered a tunnel under the pavement. Oh, it was dark, quite as dark as it was in the box at home. 'Wherever am I going now?' the tin soldier wondered. 'Yes, it must be the goblin's doing. Ah! If only that young lady were here with me in the boat, I wouldn't care if it were twice as dark.'

Suddenly, from its home in the tunnel, out rushed a large water-rat. 'Have you a passport?' it demanded. 'No entry without a passport!'

But the tin soldier said never a word; he only gripped his musket more tightly than ever. The boat rushed onwards, and behind it rushed the rat in fast pursuit. Ugh! How it ground its teeth, and yelled to the sticks and straws, 'Stop him! Stop

him! He hasn't paid his toll! He hasn't shown his passport!'

There was no stopping the boat, though, for the stream ran stronger and stronger. The tin soldier could just see a bright glimpse of daylight far ahead where the end of the tunnel must be, but at the same time he heard a roaring noise which well might have frightened a bolder man. Just imagine! At the end of the tunnel the stream thundered down into a great canal. It was as dreadful for him as a plunge down a giant waterfall would be for us.

But how could he stop? Already he was close to

the terrible edge. The boat raced on, and the poor tin soldier held himself as stiffly as he could – no one could say of him that he even blinked an eye.

Suddenly the little vessel whirled round three or four times, and filled with water right to the brim; what could it do but sink! The tin soldier stood in water up to his neck; deeper and deeper sank the boat, softer and softer grew the paper, until at last the water closed over the soldier's head. He thought of the lovely little dancer whom he would never see again, and in his ears rang the words of a song:

'Onward, onward, warrior brave!
Fear not danger, nor the grave.'

Then the paper boat collapsed entirely. Out fell the tin soldier – and he was promptly swallowed up by a fish.

Oh, how dark it was in the fish's stomach! It was even worse than the tunnel, and very much more cramped. But the tin soldier's courage remained unchanged; there he lay, as steadfast as ever, his musket still at his shoulder. The fish swam wildly about, twisted and turned, and then became quite still. Something flashed through like a streak of lightning – then all around was cheerful daylight, and a voice cried out, 'The tin soldier!'

The fish had been caught, taken to market, sold and carried into the kitchen, where the cook had cut it open with a large knife. Now she picked up the soldier, holding him round his waist between her finger and thumb, and took him into the living room, so that all the family could see the remarkable character who had travelled about inside a fish. But the tin soldier was not at all proud. They stood him up on the table, and there – well, the world is full of wonders! – he saw that he was in the very same room where his adventures had started; there were the very same children; there were the very same toys; there was the fine paper castle with the graceful little dancer at the door. She was still poised on one leg, with the other raised high in the air. Ah, she was steadfast too. The tin soldier was deeply moved; he would have liked to weep tin tears, only that would not have been soldierly behaviour. He looked at her, and she looked at him, but not a word passed between them.

And then a strange thing happened. One of the small boys picked up the tin soldier and threw him into the stove. He had no reason for doing this; it must have been the snuff-box goblin's fault.

The tin soldier stood framed in a blaze of light. The heat was intense, but whether this came from the fire or his burning love, he could not tell. His bright colours were now gone – but whether they had been washed away by his journey, or through his sorrow, none could say. He looked at the pretty little dancer, and she looked at him; he felt that he was melting away, but he still stood steadfast, shouldering arms. Suddenly the door flew open; a gust of air caught the little paper girl, and she flew like a sylph right into the stove, straight to the waiting tin soldier; there she flashed into flame and vanished.

The soldier presently melted down to a lump of tin, and the next day, when the maid raked out the ashes she found him – in the shape of a little tin heart. And the dancer? All that they found was her sequin, and that was as black as soot.

The Nightingale

You know, of course, that in China the Emperor is a Chinaman, and all the people around him are Chinese too. This story happened many years ago, but that's exactly why you should hear it now, before it is forgotten.

The Emperor's palace was the finest in the world, entirely made of the rarest porcelain – absolutely beyond price, but so fragile and delicate that you had to take the greatest care when you moved about. The palace garden was full of marvellous flowers, never seen anywhere else; the loveliest of all had little silver bells tied to them – tinkle, tinkle – to make sure that nobody passed without noticing.

Yes, everything in the Emperor's garden was wonderfully planned, and it stretched so far that even the gardener had no idea where it ended. If you kept on walking you would find yourself in a most beautiful forest with towering trees and very deep lakes. This forest went right down to the sea, which was blue and deep; great ships could sail right in under the high branches of the trees. In these branches lived a nightingale, which sang so sweetly that even the poor fisherman, with all his cares, would stop while casting his nets each night, to listen. 'Ah, it's a treat to hear it,' he would say. But then he would have to get on with his work and so would forget the bird. Yet the following night, as soon as the nightingale sang again, the fisherman would look up from his nets and say once more: 'Ah, it's a treat to hear it.'

From every country in the world travellers came to admire the Emperor's city, his palace and his garden. But as soon as they heard the nightingale, they would all declare, 'Now *that's* the best thing of all!' And when they were back at home these travellers would go on talking about the bird. Learned men wrote books about the city and the palace and the garden, but the nightingale was praised above all other marvels, and poets wrote thrilling poems about the bird in the forest near the sea.

These books were read all over the world, and one day some of them reached the Emperor too. There he sat in his golden chair, reading and reading; now and then he nodded his head. He was pleased to see such splendid descriptions of his realm. Then he came to the sentence – 'But, with all these wonders, nothing can match the nightingale.'

'What's this!' said the Emperor. 'The nightingale? Why, I've never heard of it. Just imagine! The things one can learn from books!'

So he sent for his lord-in-waiting. 'I see in this

book that we have a most remarkable bird called a nightingale,' said the Emperor. 'It's supposed to be the finest thing in my vast empire. Why has no one ever told me about it?'

'Well,' said the lord-in-waiting, 'I have never heard anyone mention the creature. Certainly it has never been presented at court.'

'It is my wish that it comes here tonight and sings to me,' said the Emperor. 'It's a disgrace that the whole world knows what I possess – and I don't.'

'I have never heard it mentioned,' repeated the lord-in-waiting. 'But I'll look for it – I'll find it.'

Yes, but where? The lord-in-waiting ran up

and down all the stairs, through all the halls and passages, but of all the people he met, not one had ever heard of the nightingale. So he hurried back to the Emperor and said that it must be a tale invented by the writers of those books. 'Your Imperial Majesty must not believe all that appears in print. The things these authors invent! It's a real black art!'

'But the book where I learnt about the bird,' said the Emperor, 'was sent to me by the high and mighty Emperor of Japan, so it can't be untrue. I *will* hear the nightingale! I'm determined to hear it tonight.'

'Tsing-pe!' said the lord-in-waiting, and once more he ran up and down all the staircases and through all the halls and passages; half the court ran with him.

At last they came across a poor little girl in the kitchen. 'The nightingale?' she said. 'My goodness, yes, of course I know it. How that bird can sing! Most evenings, after work, they let me take home a few left-over scraps for my sick mother; she lives by the lake at the other side of the wood. And when I am on my way back, and feeling tired, I sit down for a while and listen. Then I hear the nightingale.'

'Little kitchen-girl!' said the lord-in-waiting, 'I shall guarantee you a permanent kitchen appointment and permission to watch the Emperor dining, if only you will lead us to the nightingale. Its presence is commanded at court this very evening.'

So they set out for the forest where the nightingale usually sang; quite half the court joined in the expedition. As they trailed along, a cow began to moo.

'Oh!' exclaimed a court page. 'Now we can hear it! For such a small creature it makes an extraordinarily powerful noise. But – do you know – I'm sure I have heard it before.'

'No, no, that's a cow mooing,' said the little kitchen-maid. 'We've still a long way to go.'

Some frogs began croaking in the pond. 'Glorious!' said the Emperor's chaplain. 'Now I hear the song! It's just like tiny church bells!'

'No – those are frogs,' said the little kitchen-maid. 'But I think we'll hear her any minute now.'

Then the nightingale began to sing. 'There she is,' said the girl. 'Listen! Look! – there she sits.' And she pointed to a little grey bird up among the branches.

'Is it possible?' said the lord-in-waiting. 'I would never have thought it. How ordinary the creature looks! How plain! Perhaps it has lost its colour at the sight of all these distinguished visitors.'

'Little nightingale!' the kitchen-maid called. 'Our gracious Emperor would very much like you to sing for him.'

'With the greatest of pleasure,' said the nightingale, and she sang so beautifully that it was a delight to hear.

'It sounds just like glass bells,' said the lord-in-waiting. 'I can't imagine why we have never heard it before. It'll be a great hit at court!'

'Shall I sing once again for the Emperor?' said the nightingale, for she thought that the Emperor was one of these visitors.

'Most excellent nightingale,' said the lord-in-waiting, 'I have the honour and pleasure to summon you to a concert this evening at the palace, where you will enchant his Imperial Majesty with your delightful song.'

'It sounds best out in the green forest,' said the nightingale. Still, she went along willingly enough when she heard that the Emperor wished it.

Meanwhile, what a cleaning and polishing was going on at the palace. The porcelain walls and floor gleamed and sparkled in the light of thousands of golden lamps. Right in the middle of the great hall, where the Emperor sat, a golden perch was set up; this was for the nightingale. Everyone in the court was there; the little kitchen-maid was allowed to stand behind the door, for now she had the official title of Genuine Maid of the Kitchen. All eyes were turned on the little grey bird as the Emperor nodded at her to begin.

Then the nightingale sang so beautifully that tears came to the Emperor's eyes and rolled right down his cheeks; and she sang on even more thrillingly, so that every note went straight to his heart. The Emperor was greatly pleased; the nightingale, he declared, should have his golden slipper to wear round her neck. But she thanked him and refused, for she had already had her reward. 'I have seen tears in the Emperor's eyes – can any gift be greater than that? An Emperor's tears have a strange power. I have had pay enough.' And then she sang yet another song in her ravishing voice.

'Very saucy; very amusing; the creature is quite a flirt,' said the court ladies; and they filled their mouths with water to make a gurgling sound. Why shouldn't they be nightingales too? Even the lackeys and chambermaids nodded their approval, and that means a great deal, for they are the hardest of all to satisfy. No doubt about it, the nightingale really was a hit.

She was now to remain at court and to have her own cage, with permission to take the air twice in the daytime and once each night. With her on each excursion went twelve attendants, each one holding firmly on to a silk ribbon tied to the bird's leg. No, there was not much fun in these outings.

One day a large parcel arrived for the Emperor. On it was written one word – NIGHTINGALE.

'Why, here's a new book about our famous bird!' said the Emperor. But it was not a book; it was a little mechanical toy in a box, a clockwork nightingale. It was made to look like the real one but it was covered all over with diamonds, rubies and sapphires. If you wound it up it would sing one of the songs that the real bird sang, and its

tail would go up and down, glittering with silver and gold. Round its neck hung a ribbon on which was written: 'The Emperor of Japan's nightingale is a poor thing beside the nightingale of the Emperor of China.'

'How delightful!' everyone said. And the messenger who had brought the bird was given the title of Chief Imperial Bringer of Nightingales. 'Now they must sing together – what a duet that will be!'

So the two birds had to sing together, but it was not a success. The trouble was that the real nightingale sang in her own way, and the other bird's song came out of a machine. 'There's nothing to be ashamed of in that,' said the Master of the Imperial Music. 'It keeps excellent time – in fact, it could be one of my own pupils.'

So the clockwork bird was set to sing alone. It pleased the court quite as much as the real one and of course it was a great deal prettier to look at, glittering there like a bracelet or a brooch. Over and over, thirty-three times, it sang the same tune, and yet it was not in the least tired. The courtiers would gladly have heard it a few times more, but now the Emperor thought that the real one should have a turn.

But where *was* the nightingale? She had flown out of the open window, away to her own green forest, and no one had noticed.

'Tut, tut, tut!' said the Emperor. 'What's the meaning of this!' And the courtiers muttered and frowned – 'Still, we have the better bird here,' they added, and the clockwork bird had to sing its song again. That was the thirty-fourth time they had heard it, but they weren't quite sure of it even yet. It was a difficult tune to learn. And the Master of the Imperial Music praised the bird in the highest terms; it was superior to the living nightingale not only in its outward appearance – all those sparkling jewels – but in its internal workings too. 'You see, ladies and gentlemen, and above all Your Imperial Majesty, with the real nightingale you can never tell what will happen, but with the clockwork bird you can be certain; everything is clear; you can open it and see how the thoughts are arranged, how each note must precisely follow the one before.'

'Why, that's just what I was thinking,' one and another agreed. And the following Sunday the Master of the Imperial Music was allowed to give a public display of the bird to the ordinary people. They too must hear it sing, the Emperor declared. And hear it they did, and were as intoxicated by it as if they had made themselves tipsy with drinking tea, an ancient Chinese custom. They all said, 'Ah!' and held up their forefingers in the air, and nodded their heads.

But the poor fisherman, who had heard the real nightingale, said: 'It's pretty enough – sounds quite like the bird too . . . Yet there's something kind of missing, I don't know what.'

The real nightingale was banished from the Emperor's realm.

The artificial bird was awarded a special place on a silk cushion close to the Emperor's bed; piled around were all the gifts it had been given, all the gold and jewels. It was honoured with the title of High Imperial Minstrel of the Bedside Table, Class One on the Left, for even an Emperor keeps his heart on the left. The Master of the Imperial Music wrote a solemn work in twenty-five volumes about the mechanical bird. It was extremely long and learned, full of the most difficult Chinese words. But everyone pretended to have read it and to have understood it too. Nobody wished to be thought stupid!

All this went on for a whole year, until the Emperor, his court, and the rest of the Chinese people knew by heart every little trill and cluck in the toy bird's song; but for that very reason they liked it all the more. They could join in the song themselves, and this they did. The street boys went about singing *Zirril, zirril, kluk, kluk, kluk,* and the Emperor sang it too – a delightful noise, no doubt about that.

But one evening, just as the clockwork bird was singing away and the Emperor was lying in bed listening to it, something went 'Snap!' inside the bird. Whirr-rr-rr! The wheels went whizzing round and the music stopped. The Emperor leapt out of bed and sent for his own doctor. But what was the use of that? So they went and fetched the watchmaker and after a lot of muttering and poking about he managed to patch up the bird after a fashion. But he warned them that it would have to be used very sparingly; the bearings were almost worn away and it would be impossible to replace them without ruining the sound.

That was a dreadful blow! They dared not let the bird sing more than once a year, and even that was taking a risk. However, on these annual occasions the Master of the Imperial Music would make a speech full of difficult words, saying that the bird was just as good as ever – and so of course, since he said so, it *was* just as good as ever.

Five years passed, and a great sorrow fell upon

the land. The people were very fond of their Emperor but now he was gravely ill, and was not expected to live. A new Emperor had already been chosen, and crowds stood outside in the street and asked the lord-in-waiting for news. How was the Emperor? The lord-in-waiting shook his head.

Cold and pale the Emperor lay in his royal bed. Indeed, the whole court now believed him gone, and went running off to greet his successor. The servants of the bedchamber ran out to gossip; the palace maids held a big coffee party. In all the halls and corridors black cloth had been laid down to dull the sound of footsteps, so the whole palace seemed very, very still.

But the Emperor was not yet dead. Pale and unmoving he lay in his magnificent bed with its long velvet curtains and heavy tassels of gold. Through a high open window the moon shone down on the Emperor and the artificial bird.

The poor Emperor could hardly breathe; he felt as if something were sitting on his heart. He opened his eyes and saw that Death was seated there. Death was wearing the Emperor's golden crown; in one hand he held the Imperial golden sword, in the other, the splendid Imperial banner. And out of the folds of the great velvet curtains, strange faces pushed and peeped; some were hideous, others lovely and kind. They were the Emperor's evil and good deeds, looking back at him, as Death sat on his heart.

'Do you remember . . .?' 'Do you remember . . .?'

came the rustling whispers, one after another. And they told and recalled so many things that the sweat at last broke out on the Emperor's forehead.

'I never knew – I never realized,' he cried. 'Music – music! Beat the great drum of China! Save me from those voices!'

But the voices did not stop. On and on they went while Death nodded like a mandarin at everything that was said.

'Music! Let me have music!' begged the Emperor. 'Beautiful little golden bird, sing – I ask you, sing! I have given you gold and precious things; I hung my golden slipper about your neck with my own hands. Sing! – I beseech you – sing!'

But the bird was silent; there was no one to wind it up, and unless it was wound it had no voice. And Death went on gazing at the Emperor out of his great empty eye sockets. Everything was still, terribly still.

Then, all at once, close by the window, the loveliest song rang out. It came from the living nightingale which had flown to a branch outside. Hearing of the Emperor's need, the little bird had returned to bring him comfort and hope.

As she sang, the ghostly forms grew more and more shadowy, until they thinned away into nothing. The blood began to flow faster through the Emperor's body. Death himself was held by the song. 'Sing more – sing more, little nightingale,' said Death.

'Yes, if you will give me the great gold sword . . . Yes, if you will give me the rich banner . . . Yes, if you will give me the Emperor's crown.'

And Death gave up each of the treasures in return for a song, and the nightingale went on singing. She sang of the quiet churchyard where the white roses grow, where the elder-flowers smell so sweetly, where the fresh grass is kept green by the tears of those who mourn. Then Death was filled with a great longing for his garden, and he floated out of the window like a cold white mist.

'Thank you, thank you,' said the Emperor. 'You heavenly little bird, I know who you are. I banished you from my realm, and yet you alone came to my need, and drove the dreadful phantoms from my bed, and freed my heart from Death. How can I reward you?'

'You *have* rewarded me,' said the nightingale. 'When I first sang to you, tears came to your eyes and that gift I cannot forget. These are the jewels that cannot be bought or sold. But now you must sleep and grow well and strong. Listen, I will sing to you.'

And she sang, and the Emperor fell into a sweet refreshing sleep.

The sun was shining on him through the window when he woke, restored, all his illness, all his weakness gone. None of his servants had yet looked in; they all thought that he was dead. But the nightingale was still there, singing.

'You must stay with me always,' said the Emperor. 'You need sing only when you wish. And as for the clockwork bird, I'll break that into a thousand pieces.

'Don't do that,' said the nightingale. 'It has done what it could for you. Keep it as you did before. I can't make my home in a palace, but let me come and go as I wish, and then, in the evenings, I'll sit outside on that branch by the window and sing for you. I shall bring you happiness, but also serious thoughts. I shall sing about those in your realm who are joyful, and those who are sad. I shall sing of the good and evil that are all around, yet have always been hidden from you. The little bird flies far and wide, to the poor fisherman, to the labourer's cottage, to so many who are far removed from you and your splendid court. I love your heart more than your crown – and yet the crown has some magic about it. Yes, I will come – but one thing you must promise.'

'Anything!' said the Emperor. He had risen and put on his Imperial robes, and was holding the heavy golden sword against his heart.

'The one thing I ask of you is this. Tell no one that you have a little bird for a friend who tells you everything. It's best to keep it a secret.'

And with that, the nightingale flew away.

The servants came in to see their dead master. Well – there they stood!

'Good morning,' said the Emperor.

The Ugly Duckling

It was so delightful in the country. The air was full of summer; the corn was yellow; the oats were ripe; the haystacks in the meadows looked like little hills of grass, and there the stork strutted about on his long red legs. All round the open fields were woods and forests, and within these were deep cool lakes. Yes, it was really delightful in the countryside. And there, in the bright sunshine, stood an old manor house surrounded by a moat. Great dock leaves grew from the wall as far down as the water; some of them so big that little children could stand upright underneath them. In their shade, you might think yourself in a tiny secret forest of your own.

This was where a duck sat on her nest and waited for her ducklings to hatch out. She was becoming rather tired of sitting there, though, for the ducklings took so long to come; as for visitors, she hardly ever had any; the other ducks preferred swimming in the moat to dropping in under the dock leaves for a chat.

But at last the eggs began to crack, one after another. 'Peep, peep!' The nest was full of little birds poking their heads from the shell.

'Quack, quack!' said the mother. 'Quick, quick!' So the little things came out as fast as they could, and stared all round their leafy green shelter; and their mother let them look as much as they liked, for green is good for the eyes.

'How big the world is!' the young ones said. And certainly they had much more space now than they had inside the egg.

'Do you suppose that this is all the world, you foolish little creatures?' said their mother. 'Why – the world stretches out far beyond the other side of the garden, right into the parson's field. Though, to be sure, I have never been there myself. You *are* all here now, aren't you?' She got up from the nest. 'No, you're not. There's still the biggest egg. How much longer is it going to be? I'm really tired of this business, I can tell you.' And down she sat again.

'Well, how are things going?' asked an old duck, who had come to pay a call.

'This egg is taking a dreadfully long time,' said the mother duck. 'It just won't hatch! But do look at the others; they are the prettiest little ducklings I have ever seen, the living image of their father, too – that wretch, who never comes to visit me!'

'Let me look at the egg,' said the old duck. 'Ah! Take my word for it, that's a turkey's egg. I was once played the same trick, and the trouble I had with the young ones! Being turkeys, they were afraid of the water, and I *couldn't* get them to go in. I quacked and scolded, but it was no use. Let me see. Yes, that's a turkey's egg. Just let it be, and go off and teach the rest to swim.'

'Well, I'll sit on it a bit longer,' said the duck. 'As I have sat so long, I may as well finish off the job.'

'Oh well, please yourself,' said the old duck, and she went away.

At last the big egg cracked. 'Peep, peep,' said the young one as he tumbled out. But how big and ugly he was! The mother looked at him. 'That's a terribly big duckling,' she thought. 'Can he be a turkey chick after all? Well, we shall soon find out; into the water he shall go, even if I have to push him in myself.'

The next day the weather was beautiful, and

the mother duck came out with all her young ones and went down to the moat. Splash! In she went. 'Quack, quack!' she called, and one after another the ducklings plopped in. The water went over their heads, but they rose up again in a moment, and were soon swimming busily. Their feet moved of their own accord, and there they all were, out in the water – even the ugly grey one was swimming with them.

'No, that's no turkey,' the mother said. 'Look how well he uses his legs, and how straight he holds himself. He's my own child, no doubt about it. Really, he is quite handsome if you look at him properly. Quack, quack! Come along with me, children; I'll take you into the world and introduce you to the other farm birds; but mind you stay close to me, so that no one treads on you. And keep a careful look out for the cat.'

So they went into the poultry-yard. There was a horrible noise and commotion there, for two families were squabbling over the head of an eel – and then the cat got it after all.

'That's the way of the world,' said the mother duck. Her own beak watered a little, for she too would have liked the eel's head. 'Now, then, use your legs; hurry along and make a bow to the old duck over there! She is our most distinguished resident; her ancestors came from Spain, and, as you see, she has a piece of red cloth tied round her leg. That is something very special; it means that no one will get rid of her, and both man and beast must treat her with respect. Come along! Don't turn your toes in! A well-bred duckling walks with feet well apart, like father and mother. Now then! Make a bow and say "Quack!"'

The little birds did as they were told; but the other ducks in the yard looked at them and said quite loudly: 'Now we shall have to put up with all that mob, as if there weren't enough of us already. And – my goodness! What an odd-looking duckling that one is! We certainly don't want *him*!' And a duck flew at the grey one and pecked him in the neck.

'Leave him alone,' said the mother. 'He's not doing anyone any harm.'

'Yes, but he's too big, and peculiar-looking,' said the duck who had pecked at him. 'He has to be put in his place.'

'There's a fine family,' said the old duck with a piece of red cloth round her leg. 'All the children are pretty – except *that* one; he won't do at all. I do wish that the mother could make him all over again.'

'That can't be done, Your Grace,' said the mother duck. 'To be sure, he isn't handsome, but he has a nice disposition, and he swims quite as prettily as any of the others. I venture to say, he may even grow to be better-looking, and perhaps, in time, a bit smaller. He has lain too long in the egg, and that has spoilt his shape.' And she tidied the fluff on the back of his neck, and smoothed him down here and there. 'Besides,' she said, 'he's a drake, so it doesn't matter quite as much about looks. He is healthy, I'm sure, and he'll make his way in the world well enough.'

'Anyhow, the other ducklings are charming,' said the old duck. 'Well, make yourselves at home – and if you happen to come across an eel's head, you can bring it to me.'

That was only the first day; after that the grey one's plight grew worse. How wretched he felt to be so ugly! He was chased about by everyone. The ducks snapped at him; the hens too; and the girl who came to feed them shoved him with her foot. Even his brothers and sisters were against him, and kept saying: 'You ugly thing! We hope that the cat will get you!' His mother, too, would murmur, 'I wish you were far away.'

So away he went. First, he flew over the fence – and the little birds in the bushes rose up into the air with alarm. 'That's because I am so ugly,' the duckling thought, and shut his eyes. But he went on all the same. At last, he reached the wide marshes where the wild ducks lived, and he lay there all the night, for he was so tired and sad.

In the morning the wild ducks flew up and considered their new companion. 'What kind of creature are you?' they asked, and the duckling turned from one to another and greeted them as politely as he could.

'You're certainly ugly, that's a fact!' said the wild duck. 'Still, that doesn't matter so long as you don't marry into the family.'

Poor little outcast! The idea of marriage had never even entered his head. All he wanted was to lie and rest in the reeds, and to have a drink of marsh water.

There he lay for two whole days; then he was visited by a pair of wild geese – young ganders, really, for both were cock-birds. They were only recently hatched, and were as lively and saucy as could be. 'Listen, friend,' they said. 'You're so ugly that we rather like you. What about coming with us when we fly further afield? In another marsh not far from here there are some charming young wild geese, lovely girls, whose "Quack!" is worth hearing. With your funny looks, you might be quite a success with them.'

At that moment there was a Bang! Bang! and both the gay young ganders fell down dead in the reeds. The water became quite red with blood. Again Bang! Bang! – and a great flock of wild geese flew up from the rushes. A big shoot was going on. The sportsmen were stationed all round the marsh; some were even in the trees overhanging the reeds. Blue smoke drifted like clouds in and out of the dark branches and floated over the water. The dogs went splash! splash! through the mud, treading down the rushes. The poor duckling was terrified; just as he was trying to hide his head under his wing, a huge and frightful dog stood before him, with tongue hanging out of his mouth and eyes gleaming horribly. He thrust his muzzle at the duckling, showed his sharp teeth, and then – splash! He was off without touching the bird.

'Oh, thank goodness,' sighed the duckling. 'I'm so ugly that even the dog thinks twice before biting me.' And he lay quite still while shot after shot whined and banged through the reeds. The day was far on before the noise stopped; but the poor young thing dared not move even then. At last, however, he lifted up his head, peered cautiously round, then hurried away from the marsh as fast as he could. Over fields and meadows he ran, while the wind blew so keenly against him that it was hard work to get along.

Towards evening he reached a miserable hovel; it was in such a crazy state that it couldn't decide which way to tumble down, so it remained standing. The wind howled so fiercely round the duckling that he had to sit down on his tail to avoid being blown over; and the wind grew fiercer still. Then he noticed that the door had lost one of its hinges, and was hanging so crookedly that he could slip inside through the crack, and that is what he did.

In the hovel lived an old woman with a cat and a hen. The cat, whom she called Sonny, could arch his back and purr; he could give out sparks, too, but only when he was stroked the wrong way. The hen had little short legs, and so was called Chicky Short-Legs. She laid well, and the old woman was as fond of her as if she were her own child.

When morning came, the strange little visitor was noticed at once; the cat began to purr and the hen to cluck. 'What's the matter?' said the old woman, looking all about her. But her sight was none too good, so she mistook the little newcomer for a full grown bird. 'Here's a piece of luck, and no mistake,' said she. 'Now I can have duck eggs – as long as it isn't a drake. Well, we shall see.'

And the duckling was taken in on approval for three weeks; but no eggs appeared.

The cat was the master of the house and the

hen the mistress; they were always saying, 'We and the world,' for they looked on themselves as half the world, and the better half at that. The duckling thought that there might be other opinions on that matter, but the hen would not hear of it.

'Can you lay eggs?' she asked. 'No? Then kindly keep your views to yourself!'

The cat asked, 'Can you arch your back and purr, or give out sparks? No? Then you had better keep quiet while sensible people are talking.'

So the duckling sat in a corner and moped. Thoughts of fresh air and sunshine came into his mind and then, an extraordinary longing seized him to float on the water. At last, he could not help telling the hen about it.

'What a preposterous notion!' she exclaimed. 'The trouble with you is that you have nothing to do; that's why you get these fancies. Just lay a few eggs, or practise purring, and they'll pass off.'

'But it is so delicious to float on the water,' said the duckling. 'It is so lovely to put down your head and dive to the bottom.'

'That *must* be delightful!' said the hen sarcastically. 'You must be out of your mind! Ask the cat – he's the cleverest person I know – if *he* likes floating on the water, or diving to the bottom. Never mind my opinion: ask our mistress, the old woman; there's no one wiser in the whole world. Do you imagine that *she* wants to float or put her head under water?'

'You don't understand,' said the duckling, sadly.

'Well, if we don't understand you, nobody will. You'll never be as wise as the cat and the old woman, to say nothing of myself. Don't give yourself airs, child, but be thankful for all the good things that have been done for you. Haven't you found a warm room and elegant company, from whom you can learn plenty if you listen? But all you do is talk nonsense; you're not even cheerful to be with. Believe me, I mean this for your good. Now do make an effort to lay some eggs, or at least learn to purr and give out sparks.'

'I think I had better go out into the wide world,' said the duckling.

'All right, do,' said the hen.

So the duckling went. He floated on the water, and dived below the surface; but it seemed to him that other ducks ignored him because of his ugliness.

Now autumn came; the leaves in the wood turned brown and yellow; the wind caught them and whirled them madly round; the very sky looked chill; the clouds hung heavy with hail and snow, and the raven, perched on the fence, cried 'Caw! Caw!' because of the cold. Even to look at the scene was enough to make you shiver. It was a hard time for the duckling too.

One evening, as the sky flamed with the setting sun, a flock of marvellous great birds rose out of the rushes. The duckling had never seen any birds so beautiful. They were brilliantly white, with long graceful necks – indeed, they were swans; uttering a strange sound, they spread their splendid wings and flew far away to warmer lands and lakes which did not freeze. High in the air they soared, and the ugly duckling was filled with a wild excitement; he turned round and round in the water like a wheel, and called out in a voice so loud and strange that it quite frightened him. Oh, he would never forget those wonderful birds, those fortunate birds! As soon as the last was out of sight, he dived right down to the bottom of the water, and when he came up again he was almost frantic. He did not know what the birds were called; he did not know where they had come from, nor where they were flying – but he felt more deeply drawn to them than to anything he had ever known.

The winter grew colder still. The duckling had to swim round and round in the water to keep it from freezing over; but every night the ice-free part became smaller. Then he had to use his feet all the time to break up the surface; at last, however, he was quite worn out. He lay still and was frozen fast in the ice.

Early next morning a peasant came by. Seeing the bird, he went out, broke up the ice with his wooden clogs, and carried him home to his wife. Presently the duckling came to life again. The children wanted to play with him, but he thought that they meant to hurt him, and in his fright he flew into the milk-pail. The milk splashed all over the room; the woman shrieked and threw up her hands – then he flew into the butter tub, then into the flour barrel, and out again. Goodness, what a sight he was! The woman, still screaming, hit out at him with the fire-tongs; the children, laughing and shrieking, tumbled over one another as they tried to grab the little creature. Luckily, the door stood open; out he rushed into the bushes and the new-fallen snow, and lay there in a kind of swoon.

But it would be too sad to tell you of all the hardships and miseries that he had to go through during that cruel winter. One day he was huddling among the reeds in the marsh when the sun began to send down warm rays again; the larks started their song; how glorious! It was spring. The duckling raised his wings. They seemed stronger than before, and carried him swiftly away; before he realized what was happening, he was in a lovely garden full of apple-trees in blossom, and where sweet-smelling lilac hung on its long boughs right down to the winding stream. And then, directly in front of him, out of the leafy shadows, came three magnificent white swans, ruffling their feathers as they floated lightly over the water. The duckling recognized the wonderful birds, and a strange sadness came over him.

'I will fly to those noble birds, even though they may peck me to death for daring to come near them, an ugly thing like me. But I don't care – better to be killed by such splendid creatures than to be pecked by ducks and hens and kicked by the poultry-yard girl – or be left to suffer another winter like the last.' So he flew out to the open water, and swam towards the glorious swans. They saw him, and came speeding towards him, ruffling their plumage.

'Yes, kill me,' said the poor creature, bowing his head right down to the water as he waited for his end. Yet what did he see reflected below? He beheld his own likeness – but he was no longer an awkward ugly dark grey bird. He was like the proud white birds about him; he was a swan.

It doesn't matter if you are born in a duck-yard, so long as you come from a swan's egg.

He felt glad that he had suffered so much hardship and trouble, for now he could value his good fortune and the home he had found at last. The stately swans swam round him, and stroked him admiringly with their beaks. Some little children came into the garden and threw bread into the water, and the smallest of all cried joyfully: 'There's a new one!' And the others called out in delight, 'Yes, a new swan has come!' They clapped their hands and danced about with pleasure: then they ran to tell their father and mother. More bread and cake were thrown into the water, and everyone said: 'The new one is the most beautiful of all. Look how handsome he is, that young one there.' And the older swans bowed before him.

He felt quite shy, and hid his head under his wing; he did not know what to do. He was almost too happy, yet he was not proud, for a good heart is never proud or vain. He remembered the time when he had been persecuted and scorned, yet now he heard everyone saying that he was the most beautiful of all these beautiful birds. The lilacs bowed their branches down to the water to greet him; the sun sent down its friendly warmth, and the young bird, his heart filled with joy, ruffled his feathers, raised his slender neck, and said, 'I never dreamt that such happiness could ever be when I was the ugly duckling.'

The Snow Queen
A Story in Seven Parts

Part the First: Which Tells of the Looking Glass and the Splinters

Listen now! We're going to begin our story. When we come to the end of it we shall know more than we do now. There was once a wicked imp, a demon, one of the very worst – he was the Devil himself. One day, there he was, laughing his head off. Why? Because he had made a magic mirror with a special power; everything good and beautiful that was reflected in it shrivelled up almost to nothing, but everything evil and ugly seemed even larger, and more hideous than it was. In this glass, the loveliest landscapes looked just like boiled spinach, and even the nicest people appeared quite horrible, or seemed to be standing on their heads, or to have no trunks to their bodies. As for their faces, they were so twisted and changed that no one could have recognized them; and, if anything holy and serious passed through someone's mind, a hideous sneering grin was shown in the glass. This was a huge joke.

All the students who attended his Demon School went around declaring that he'd achieved a miracle; now for the first time everyone could see what the world and its humans were really like. They took the mirror and ran around to the four corners of the earth, until there wasn't a place or person unharmed by the glass.

At last they fixed on a still more daring plan – to fly up to heaven, to make fun of the angels, and of God himself. The higher they flew with the mirror, the more it grimaced and twisted; they could scarcely hold on to it. Up and up they went, nearer and nearer to heaven's kingdom – until, disaster! The mirror shook so violently with its weird reflections that it sprang out of their hands and went crashing down to earth, where it burst into hundreds of millions, billions, trillions of tiny pieces. And that made matters even worse than before, for some of these pieces were hardly as big as a grain of sand. These flew here and there, all through the wide world; whoever got a speck in his eye saw everything good as bad or twisted – for every little splinter had the same power that the whole glass had. Some people even caught a splinter in their hearts, and that was horrible, for their hearts became just like lumps of ice. Some of the pieces were so big that they were used as window panes – but it didn't do to look at your friends through them. Other pieces were made into spectacles – imagine! The demon laughed till he nearly split his sides.

And, as we tell this story, little splinters of magic glass are still flying about in the air. Listen! You shall hear what happened to some of them.

Part the Second:
A Little Boy and a Little Girl

In a big city, where there are so many houses and people that there isn't room for everyone to have a garden, and so most people have to make do with flowers in pots, there once lived two poor children. But these two did have a garden a little larger than a flower pot. They were not brother and sister, but they were just as fond of each other as if they had been. Their parents were next-door neighbours; they lived in attics at the tops of next-door houses. Where the sloping roofs almost touched, a gutter ran along between; and across this, each house had a little window facing the other. You had only to step along the strip of roof to cross from window to window.

The parents each had a wooden box standing outside the window, and here they grew vegetables and herbs. They had little rose trees too, one in each box, and these grew gloriously. The pea plants trailed over the edges; the rose trees put out long branches, some twining around the windows, some bending over towards the opposite bush, making a kind of arch of leaves and flowers.

The children would often sit on their little wooden stools under the roof of roses, and talk and play and spend many a happy hour.

In the winter, of course, there was no sitting out on the roof. The windows were often thick with frost, but the two children would warm up a coin on the stove, then press it on the frozen pane; this would make a splendid peep-hole. Behind each round hole was a bright and friendly eye, one at each window. These were the eyes of the little boy and the little girl; his name was Kay and hers was Gerda. In summer they could be together

with a single jump, but in winter they had first to climb all the way down one lot of stairs, then up another – while outside the snow fell fast.

'Those are the white bees swarming,' said the old grandmother.

'Have they a queen too?' asked the little boy, for he knew that real bees have.

'Yes, indeed,' said the grandmother. 'Wherever the flakes swarm most thickly, there she flies; she is the largest of them all. She never lies still on the ground, though, but soars up once again into the black cloud. On many a winter night she flies through the streets of the town and peers in at the windows, and then they freeze into the strangest patterns, like stars and flowers.'

'Yes, I've seen that!' both children cried at once, knowing now that it must be true.

'Could the Snow Queen come in here?' asked the little girl.

'Just let her try!' said the boy. 'I'll put her on the hot stove and then she'll melt.'

But the grandmother smoothed his hair, and told them other stories.

In the evening, when little Kay was back at home and half undressed, he climbed on to the chair by the window and looked out through the little hole. A few snowflakes were drifting outside; then one of these, much larger than the rest, settled on the edge of the window-box outside. This snowflake grew and grew until it seemed to take the shape of a lady dressed in the finest white gauze, which was in fact made up of millions of tiny starlike flakes. She was so beautiful, wonderfully delicate and grand; but she was of ice all through, dazzling, glittering ice – and yet she was alive. Her eyes blazed out like two bright stars, but there was no peace or rest in them. Now she nodded towards the window, and beckoned with her hand. The little boy was frightened and jumped down from the chair, and then he thought he saw a great bird go flying past.

The next day was clear and frosty; after that the thaw began; then it was spring. The sun shone; the first green shoots appeared; swallows built their nests; the windows were thrown open and the two children sat once more in their little roof garden.

The roses were so beautiful that summer, more than ever before. The little girl had learnt a hymn which had a line about roses, and these made her think of her own. She sang the verse to the little boy, and he sang it too:

'In the vale the rose grows wild;
Children play all the day –
One of them is the Christ-child.'

How lovely the summer was. The rose garden seemed as if it would never stop flowering.

Kay and Gerda were sitting looking at a picture book of birds and animals, and then – just as the clock in the great church tower began to strike five – Kay said, 'Oh! Something pricked me in my heart! Oh! Now I've got something in my eye!'

The little girl put her arm round his neck, and he blinked his eyes. But no, there was nothing to be seen.

'I think it's gone,' he said. But it hadn't. It was one of those tiny splinters from the demon's looking-glass – I'm sure you remember it. Poor Kay! He had got another piece right in his heart, which would soon be like a lump of ice. He didn't feel it hurting now, but it was there all right.

'Why are you crying?' he asked. 'It makes you look horribly ugly. There's nothing the matter with me. Ugh!' he cried suddenly. 'That rose has a worm in it. And look at that one – it's crooked. They're rotten, all of them. So are the boxes, too.' And then he kicked the box hard, and tore off the two roses.

'Kay, what are you doing?' cried the little girl. And when he saw how frightened she was, he tore off a third rose, and ran in at his window, away from his little friend Gerda.

After that, when she brought out the picture book, he said that it was baby-stuff. When the grandmother told them stories, he would always find fault, and argue. He would even walk close behind her, put on spectacles, and mimic her way of talking. It was so well done that it made the people laugh. Soon he could mimic the ways of everyone in the street, especially if they were odd or unpleasant. People used to say, 'Oh, he's clever, that boy!' But all this came from the splinters of glass in his eye and in his heart; they made him tease even little Gerda, who loved him more than anything in the world.

His games had become quite different now; they were so scientific and practical. One winter's day, as the snowflakes drifted down, he brought out a magnifying glass, then held out the corner of his blue jacket to catch some falling flakes.

'Now look through the glass, Gerda,' he said. And she saw that every flake was very much larger, and looked like a splendid flower or a ten-pointed star. It was certainly a wonderful sight. 'Look at that pattern – isn't it marvellous!' said Kay. 'These are much more interesting than real flowers – and there isn't a single fault in them. They're perfect – if only they didn't melt.'

A little later Kay came back wearing big gloves and carrying his sledge on his back. He shouted into Gerda's ear: 'They're letting me go tobogganing in the town square where the others are playing!' And away he went.

Out in the square the boldest boys could often tie their sledges to farmers' carts, and so be pulled along for quite a ride. It was enormous fun. This time, while their games were in full swing, a very large sledge arrived; it was painted white all over, and in it sat a figure muffled up in a white fur cloak and wearing a white fur hat. This sledge drove twice round the square; but, moving quickly, Kay managed to fix his own sledge behind it, and a swift ride began. The big sledge went faster and faster, then turned off into the next street. The driver looked round and nodded to Kay in the friendliest fashion, just as if they had always known each other. Every time that Kay thought of unfastening his sledge, the driver would turn and nod to him again, so he kept still. On they drove, straight out of the city gates. And now the snow began to fall so thick and fast that the little boy couldn't even see his hand in front of him as they rushed along. At last he *did* manage to untie the rope but it was of no use; his little sledge still clung to the big one, and they sped along like the wind. He cried out at the top of his voice, but no one heard him; the snow fell, and the sledge raced on. From time to time it seemed to jump, as if they were going over dykes and hedges. Terror seized him; he tried to say the Lord's Prayer, but all he could remember was the multiplication table.

The snowflakes grew bigger and bigger, until at last they looked like great white birds. All at once they swerved to one side; the sledge came to a halt, and the driver stood up. The white fur cloak and cap were all of snow and the driver – ah, she was a lady, tall and slender, dazzlingly white! She was the Snow Queen herself.

'We've come far and fast,' she said. 'But you must be frozen. Creep under my bearskin cloak.' She put him beside her in the sledge and wrapped the cloak around him; he felt as if he were sinking into a snowdrift. 'Are you still cold?' she asked, and she kissed him on the forehead. Ah-h-h! Her kiss was colder than ice; it went straight to his heart, which was already half way to being a lump of ice. He felt as if he were dying, but only for a moment. Then he felt perfectly well, and no longer noticed the cold.

'My sledge! Don't forget my sledge!' That was the first thought that came to him. So it was tied to one of the big white birds, which flew along with the little sledge at its back. The Snow Queen kissed Kay once again, and after that he had no memory of Gerda and grandmother, nor of anyone at home.

'Now I must give you no more kisses,' said the Snow Queen, 'or you will be kissed to death.'

Kay looked at her. She was so beautiful; he could not imagine a wiser, lovelier face. She no longer seemed to him to be made of ice, as she once had seemed when she came to the attic window and waved to him. Now in his eyes she was perfect, and he felt no fear. He told her that he could do mental arithmetic, and fractions too; that he knew the square miles of all the principal countries, and the number of inhabitants. As he talked she smiled at him, until he began to think that what he knew was, after all, not quite so much. And he looked up into the vast expanse of the sky, as they rose up high, and she flew with him over the dark clouds, while the storm-wind whistled and raved, making him think of ballads of olden time. Over forest and lake they flew, over sea and land; beneath them screamed the icy blast; the wolves howled, the snow glittered; the black crows soared across the plains, cawing as they went. But high over all shone the great clear silver moon, and Kay gazed up at it all through the long long winter night. During the day he slept at the Snow Queen's feet.

Part the Third: The Enchanted Flower Garden of the Old Woman Who Understood Magic

But what of little Gerda when Kay did not return? Where could he be? No one knew; no one had any idea. The only thing that the boys could say was that they had seen him tie his little sledge to a big one, which drove out into the street and through the city gate. But who could tell what happened after that? There was great grief in the town; little Gerda wept many tears. Then people began to say that he must be dead, that he had fallen into the river that flowed past the city walls. Oh, what a long dark winter it was!

At last came the spring, and the first warm sunshine.

'Kay is dead and gone,' said little Gerda.

'*I* don't believe it,' said the sunshine.

'He is dead and gone,' she said to the swallows.

'*I* don't believe it,' declared each of the

swallows. And at last little Gerda didn't believe it either.

'I will put on my new red shoes,' she said one morning, 'the ones Kay has never seen, and I'll go down and ask the river.'

It was still very early when she kissed her sleeping grandmother, put on the red shoes, and walked all alone through the city gate and down to the river.

'Is it true that you have taken my little playmate?' she said. 'I'll give you my red shoes if you'll let me have him back.'

The waves, she thought, nodded back to her very strangely. So she took off her red shoes, the most precious things she owned, and threw them into the water. But they fell close to the bank, and the little waves carried them straight back to her. It seemed just as if the river would not accept her dearest possession because it hadn't taken little Kay. But then Gerda felt that perhaps she hadn't thrown the shoes out far enough, so she climbed into a boat that lay among the rushes, and went to the further end of it, and threw the shoes again. But the boat had not been moored fast, and the movement made it float away from the shore. It began to glide away, gathering speed all the time.

At this little Gerda was very much frightened and began to cry, only nobody heard her except the sparrows, and they couldn't carry her ashore. But they flew along the bank, singing as if to comfort her: 'Here we are! Here we are!' On sped the boat while little Gerda sat quite still in her stockinged feet. Her red shoes floated behind, but they couldn't catch the boat, which was now moving faster and faster.

The scene was pretty enough on both sides of the water; there were lovely flowers, old trees and grassy meadows with sheep and cows, but there wasn't a person in sight.

'Perhaps the river is carrying me to little Kay,' thought Gerda, and her spirits began to rise. She stood up, and gazed for hour after hour at the beautiful green banks. At last she came to a cherry orchard, in which stood a little house with curious red and blue windows and a thatched roof; standing outside were two wooden soldiers, presenting arms whenever anyone passed. Gerda called out to them, thinking that they were alive, but of course they gave no answer. The river seemed to be driving the boat towards the bank, and Gerda called out even more pleadingly. Then, from the cottage, came an old, old woman, leaning on a crutch-shaped stick. She wore a large sun-hat, painted all over with many kinds of lovely flowers.

'You poor little child!' said the old woman. 'How ever did you come to be on this river, so far out in the wide world?' And with that she stepped into the water, hooked the boat with her crooked stick, pulled it ashore, and lifted little Gerda down.

'Now come and tell me who you are,' said she, 'and how you managed to reach my house.'

So Gerda told her everything, and the old woman shook her head, and murmured, 'Hm, hm!' And when Gerda had finished her tale, and asked if she had seen little Kay, the woman said that he hadn't yet passed by, but he was sure to come; she was not to worry, but to have a taste of her cherries, and see her flowers, which were more wonderful than any picture book; every one of them had a story to tell. Then she took Gerda into the little house, and locked the door.

The windows were very high up, and the glass in them was red and yellow and blue. The daylight shone very strangely into the room with all these colours. But on the table were the most delicious cherries, and Gerda was told that she might eat as many as she liked. While she was eating, the old woman combed her hair with a golden comb, and her hair curled fair and shining round her little face that was just like a rose.

'I've often thought I would fancy a nice little girl around, just like you,' said the old woman. 'We shall get on very well together, you shall see.' And she combed away at Gerda's hair, and as she combed, the little girl was forgetting more and more her playmate Kay. For the old woman could manage a bit of magic, though she was by no means a wicked witch. She used her magic only now and then for her own pleasure – and just now her pleasure was to keep little Gerda. To make sure of this, she went out into the garden and pointed her stick at each of the lovely rose-bushes; at once, each bush sank down into the black earth, as if it had never been. For the old woman feared that if Gerda saw the roses she would think of her own in the roof-boxes, and remember little Kay, and run off to take up her journey.

This done, she took Gerda out into the flower garden. Ah, that garden – you can't imagine what magical beauty and fragrance she found there. All the flowers that you could ever bring to mind were growing together in full bloom at one time. It was better than all the picture books. Gerda jumped with joy and played there until the sun went down behind the tall cherry trees. Then she was given a lovely bed, its red silk pillows stuffed with violets, and here she slept.

When morning came she went out again to play among the flowers in the radiant sunshine, and so many days were spent. Before long she knew every separate flower, and yet, although there were so many, she felt that one was missing – only she could not think which. Then one day, as she was sitting indoors, her eyes turned to the painted flowers in the old woman's sun-hat; the loveliest of all was a rose. The old woman had quite forgotten this when she had made the real ones disappear into the ground. See what happens when you don't keep your wits about you!

'Oh!' cried Gerda. 'Why have I never seen any roses in the garden?' And she ran in and out of the flower beds, searching and searching, but not a rose was to be found. At last she sat down and cried; but her warm tears fell just where a rose tree had sunk down. At once the tree sprang up, as full of fresh flowers as when it disappeared. Gerda put her arms around it, and kissed the roses, and thought about those in the roof-garden of her home – and then she remembered Kay.

'Oh, what a lot of time I have lost!' said the little girl. 'I set out to find Kay. Do you know where he is?' she asked the roses. 'Do you think he is dead and gone?'

'No, he is not dead,' said the roses. 'We have been in the earth where the dead are, but Kay was not there.'

'Oh, thank you,' said Gerda; then she went over to the other flowers, and looked into their cups, and asked, 'Do you know where little Kay is?'

But the flowers stood in the sun, each one dreaming its own story. And Gerda listened to all the tales and dreams, but of Kay there was never a word.

What did the convolvulus say?

'High above, overlooking the narrow mountain road, stands an ancient castle. Evergreen creepers grow thickly over the old red walls; leaf by leaf they twine round the balcony where a fair young girl leans over the balustrade, gazing down at the path below. No rose on its branch is fresher and lovelier; no apple blossom that floats from the tree is more graceful and delicate. Listen – her silk dress rustles as she moves. "When will he come?" she says.'

'Is it Kay you mean?' asked little Gerda.

'I tell only my own story, my own dream,' the convolvulus answered.

What did the little snowdrop say?

'Between the trees a board hangs by two ropes; it's a swing. Two pretty little girls in snow-white dresses sit swinging; long green silk ribbons are fluttering from their hats. Their brother, who is bigger than they are, is standing up in the swing with his arm round the rope to keep himself steady, for in one hand he holds a little bowl and in the other a clay pipe; he is blowing soap bubbles. To and fro goes the swing, while the bubbles float away in a rainbow of changing colours; the last one still clings to the pipe and sways in the wind. The swing still moves, to and fro. The little black dog, as light as the bubbles, leaps up on his hind-legs; he wants to join the others on the swing. But it swoops past, out of reach, and the dog flops down, barking furiously. The children laugh; the bubbles burst. A swinging plank, a white flash of dissolving foam – that is my picture; that's my song.'

'Your story may be beautiful, but you make it sound so sad, and you don't mention little Kay at all. Hyacinths, what have you to tell?'

'There were three lovely sisters, fragile, exquisite; one wore a dress of rose-red, the second of violet-blue, the third, pure white. Hand in hand they danced by the silent lake in the clear moonlight. They were not fairies, they were children of men. A sweet scent filled the air and the girls vanished into the wood. The fragrance grew more powerful; three coffins, in which lay three lovely girls, glided from the depths of the wood, over the lake; fireflies flew around them like tiny flickering lamps. Are the dancing maidens sleeping or are they dead? Perhaps, from the scent of the flowers, they are dead, and the bells are ringing for them.'

'You make me feel dreadfully sad,' said little Gerda. 'And your own scent is so powerful that I can't help thinking of those sleeping girls. Can little Kay really be dead? The roses have been in the ground, and they say no.'

'Ding dong!' rang out the hyacinth bells. 'We're not ringing for little Kay; we don't know him. All we sing is our own song, the only one we know.'

So Gerda went to the buttercup, which shone out from its fresh green leaves. 'You are a bright little sun!' said Gerda. 'Tell me if you know where I can find my playmate.'

The buttercup shone very prettily, and looked up at Gerda. Now what song would the buttercup sing? Not one that gave her news of little Kay.

'In a small back yard the heavenly sun shone bright and warm; it was the first day of spring, and the sunbeams slid down the neighbour's white-washed wall. Near by, the first yellow flowers of spring were growing, gleaming just like gold in the golden rays. The old grandmother sat outside in her chair; her granddaughter, a poor servant girl, but pretty enough, had come home for a short visit, and now she kissed her grandmother. There was heart's gold in that kiss in the golden morning. That's all; there's my story.'

'My poor old granny!' sighed Gerda. 'I'm sure she's longing for me and grieving, just as she grieved about little Kay. But I'll soon be home again, and bring Kay with me. It's no use asking the flowers – their own tales are all they know, and they tell me nothing at all.'

She tucked up her dress so that she could run fast, and away she went. Then something struck her leg quite smartly as she leapt over it; she looked – and it was a narcissus. 'Maybe *you* have news for me,' she thought, and she bent down towards the flower.

'I see myself! I see myself!' said the narcissus. 'Ah, what a sweet perfume! High up in her attic lodging is a little ballet dancer. She stands on tiptoe, now on one leg, now on the other, and kicks out at the world. It is all in the mind, you know. Now she pours water from the kettle on to a piece of cloth – it's her dancer's bodice; cleanliness is next to godliness, as they say. Her white dress hangs on a peg; that too has been washed, then hung on the roof to dry. Now she puts it on, and round her neck she ties a saffron yellow scarf. It makes the dress seem even whiter. She raises one leg high in the air. How elegantly she stands and sways on her stalk! I see myself! I see myself!'

'That is your story, not mine,' said Gerda. 'I don't want to hear any more.' She ran to the edge of the garden. The gate was locked, but she twisted the rusty fastening until it came away; the gate flew open, and little Gerda ran out barefooted into the wide world. Three times she looked back, but nobody was following her. At last she could run no further, so she sat down on a big stone. As she gazed around her, she realized that summer was over; it was late autumn. There had been no signs of changing time in that enchanted garden, where the bright sun always shone, and flowers of every season bloomed together.

'Oh, I have lingered here too long,' said little

Gerda. 'Autumn has come; I dare not stop!' She got up from the stone and started off once more.

How tired and sore her feet were! How cold and damp was the countryside! The long willow leaves had turned quite yellow and wet with mist; they dropped off one by one. Only the thorny sloe had kept its fruit, but that was so sour that the thought of it twisted your mouth. Oh, how mournful and bleak it was in the wide world!

Part the Fourth: Prince and Princess

Gerda soon had to rest again. And there, hopping about in the snow, right in front of her, was a raven. He had been staring at her for some time, with his head on one side, then on the other. Now he greeted her: 'Caw, caw! How do, how do!' It may not have been an elegant way of speaking, but it was kindly meant. He asked her where she was going, all alone in the wide world. So she told the raven the whole of her story and asked if he had seen little Kay.

The raven nodded thoughtfully, and said, 'Could be! Could be!'

'Oh – you really think that you have some news?' cried the little girl. And she hugged the bird so tightly that she nearly squeezed him to death.

'Caw, caw! Care-ful, care-ful!' the raven said. 'I think that it may have been little Kay. But I fancy that by this time he will have forgotten you for the princess.'

'Does he live with a princess?' asked Gerda.

'Now listen and I'll tell you,' said the raven. 'But I find it so hard to talk your language. If only you understood raven-speech I could tell you better.'

'No, I never learnt that,' said Gerda, 'though my granny knew it and other strange things too. I only wish I did.'

'Well, never mind,' said the raven. 'I'll tell you as plainly as I can; you can't ask for more.' And then he related what he knew.

'In the kingdom where we are now, a princess dwells. She is extremely clever; she has read all the newspapers in the world and has forgotten them again – that's how clever she is. She was sitting on her throne the other day when she happened to hear a little song. It goes like this: *Why should I not married be? Why not? Why not? Why not?* "Well, there's something to be said for that," she thought. So she decided to find a partner, but she wanted one who could speak for himself when spoken to – one who didn't just stand and look important. That's very dull. She ordered her ladies-in-waiting to be called together – (it was done by sounding a roll of drums) – and when they heard her plan they were delighted. "What a splendid idea!" "We were thinking something of the kind just the other day!" They went on making remarks like these. All that I'm telling you is perfectly true,' said the raven. 'I've a tame sweetheart who has a free run of the palace, and I heard the tale from her.'

Need I tell you that the sweetheart was also a raven? Birds will be birds, and a raven's mate is a raven.

'The newspapers promptly came out with a border of hearts and the princess's monogram. They announced that any good-looking young man might come to the palace and meet the princess; the one who seemed most at home in the princess's company but who was also the best and most interesting talker – that was the one she meant to choose.

'Well, the suitors flocked to the palace – there never was such a crowd! But nobody won the prize, either the first day, or the next. They could all talk smartly enough when they were out in the street, but when they came through the palace gate and saw the guards in their silver uniforms, and the footmen in gold all the way up the stairs, and the great halls with their brilliant lights – they seemed to be struck dumb. And when they stood before the throne where the princess sat, they could find nothing to say but the last word she had spoken herself, and she had no wish to hear *that* again. Though once they were back in the street, it was all chatter, chatter as before.

'There was a queue stretching away right from

the city gate to the palace. I went over myself to have a look,' went on the raven.

'But Kay, little Kay!' asked Gerda. 'When did he come? Was he in that crowd?'

'Give me time! Give me time! We're coming to him! It was on the third day when a little chap appeared without horse or carriage, and stepped jauntily up to the palace. His eyes were shining, just like yours: he had fine thick flowing hair – but his clothes, I must say, were shabby.'

'That was Kay!' cried Gerda. 'Oh, I have found him at last!' And she clapped her hands with joy.

'He had a little knapsack, or bundle on his back,' said the raven.

'Ah, that must have been his sledge,' said Gerda. 'He had it when he left.'

'It may have been,' said the raven. 'I didn't study it all that closely. But I do know from my tame sweetheart that when he reached the palace gate and saw the guards in silver and the footmen in gold, he was not in the least dismayed. He only nodded pleasantly and said to them: "It must be dull work standing there; I'd sooner go inside."

'The great halls blazed with light; it was enough to make anyone feel small. The young chap's boots squeaked dreadfully, but even this didn't trouble him.'

'That's certainly Kay!' cried Gerda. 'His boots were new, I know; I heard them squeaking in my grandmother's kitchen.'

'Well, they squeaked, to be sure,' said the raven. 'But he went merrily up to the princess, who was sitting on a pearl as big as a spinning wheel; all the ladies-in-waiting, with their maids, and their maids' maids, and all the gentlemen courtiers with their serving-men, and their serving-men's serving-men were ranged around her in order.'

'But did Kay win the princess?' asked little Gerda.

'If I hadn't been a bird I would have had a try myself, betrothed or not betrothed,' the raven said. 'He is said to have spoken as well as I do when I speak in my own raven language – or so my tame sweetheart tells me. He was so lively and confident; he hadn't come to woo the princess, he declared, only to hear her wise conversation. He liked it very well, and she liked him.'

'Oh, that was certainly Kay,' said Gerda. 'He was so clever, he could do mental arithmetic with fractions! Oh, do please take me to the palace.'

'That's easily said,' replied the raven, 'but how is it to be done? I must talk to my tame sweetheart about it; she'll be able to advise us, I have no doubt, for – let me tell you – a girl like you would never be allowed to enter in the regular way.'

'Oh, I shall get in,' said Gerda. 'When Kay knows I am here he'll come straight out and fetch me.'

'Well,' said the raven, waggling his head, 'wait for me there by the stile.' And off he flew.

It was late in the evening when he returned.

'Ra-a-ax! ra-a-ax!' he cawed. 'I'm to give you my sweetheart's greetings, and here's a piece of bread from the kitchen; there's plenty there, and you must be hungry. It's impossible for you to get into the palace as you are, without even shoes on your feet; but don't cry. My sweetheart knows a little back staircase that leads to the royal bedroom, and she knows where to find the key!'

So they went into the garden, and along the avenue where the leaves were falling, leaf after leaf; then, when all the lights in the palace had gone out, one by one, the raven led little Gerda to a small back door.

Oh, how Gerda's heart beat with hope and fear! It was just as if she were about to do something wrong – yet all she wanted was to find out if the boy really *was* little Kay. Oh yes, he must be Kay; she could see him in her mind so vividly with his bright clever eyes and smooth flowing hair; she remembered the way he used to smile when they sat together at home among the roses. Oh, he would surely be glad to see her, to hear what a long way she had come for his sake, and to know how grieved they had all been at home when he never returned. She trembled with fear, and hope.

They had now reached the staircase where the tame raven was waiting; a little lamp was glimmering on a stand. Gerda curtsied, as her grandmother had taught her.

'My fiancé has spoken most charmingly of you,

my dear young lady,' said the tame raven, 'and your life-history, as we may call it, really touches the heart. If you will kindly take the lamp. I will lead the way. Straight on is best and shortest – we are not likely to meet anyone.'

'Yet I can't help feeling that someone is following behind,' said Gerda. And indeed, something did seem to rush along past her; it looked like a flight of shadows on the wall, horses with thin legs and flowing manes, huntsmen, lords and ladies on horseback.

'Those are only dreams,' said the tame raven. 'They come and take the gentry's thoughts on midnight rides and that's a good thing, for you will be able to observe them more safely while they are asleep. But I hope that you will show a thankful heart if you do rise to fame and fortune.'

'Now, now, there's no need to talk about that,' said the woodland raven.

They entered the first room, where the walls were hung with rose-coloured satin embroidered with flowers. Here, the dreams were racing past so swiftly that Gerda could not distinguish any one of the lords and ladies. Each hall that she passed through was more magnificent than the one before; then, at last, they arrived at the royal bedroom.

The ceiling was like the crown of a palm tree, with leaves of rarest crystal; and, hanging from a thick gold stem in the centre of the floor, were two beds, each in the shape of a lily. One was white, and in this lay the princess. The other was scarlet – and in this Gerda knew that she must look for little Kay. She turned one of the red leaves over, and saw a boy's brown hair. It was Kay! She cried his name aloud, holding the lamp near his face; the dreams on their wild steeds came whirling back to the sleeper; he woke – he turned his head – it was not little Kay.

No, it was not little Kay, though the prince too was a handsome boy. And now the princess looked out from the white lily bed and asked what was happening. Little Gerda wept as she told her story, but she did not forget to speak of the ravens and their kind help.

'You poor child,' said the prince and princess, and they praised the ravens, adding, though, that they must not do it again. This time, all things considered, they would be given a reward.

'Would you like to fly away free?' the princess asked. 'Or would you like a permanent place as Court Ravens, with all the odds and ends you want from the kitchens?'

Both the ravens bowed, and prudently chose the permanent place, for they had to think of their old age. 'It's a good thing to have something by for a rainy day,' they said. The prince stepped out of his bed so that Gerda could sleep in it – and who could do more than that? As Gerda slept, the dreams came flying back – but this time they looked like angels; they seemed to be drawing a sledge, on which Kay was sitting, nodding at her. But this was only a dream, and it vanished as soon as she woke.

The next day she was dressed from top to toe in silk and velvet. She was invited to stay at the palace and pass delightful days, but she begged to have just a little carriage with a horse to draw it, and a pair of boots small enough for her feet; with these she could drive out into the wide world and seek for little Kay.

She was given not only boots but a muff, and when she was ready to leave, in beautiful fine warm clothes, a new carriage of pure gold drew up before the door; on it the coat-of-arms of the royal pair glistened like a star. Coachman, footmen and outriders – for there were outriders too – all wore gold crowns. The prince and princess personally helped her into the carriage and wished her good luck. The forest raven, who had now married his sweetheart, came along for the first twelve miles or so; he sat beside her, for he could not bear travelling backwards. The tame bird stood in the gateway flapping her wings; she didn't go with them because too much rich palace fare had given her a headache. The inside of the coach was lined with iced cake and sugar candy, while the space beneath the seat was packed with fruit and ginger nuts.

'Farewell! Farewell!' cried the prince and princess, and little Gerda wept. So did the raven, and in this way they passed the first few miles. Then the raven said his own goodbye, and that was the hardest parting of them all. He flew up into a tree and flapped his black wings as long as he could see the carriage, which gleamed as bright as the sun.

Part the Fifth:
The Little Robber Girl

They drove through the dark forest, but the carriage shone like a fiery torch; it dazzled the eyes of the robber band – they could not bear it.

'It's gold! It's gold!' they roared. Then, rushing forward, they seized the horses, killed the outriders, coachman, and footmen, and dragged little Gerda out of the carriage.

'She's plump; she's a dainty dish; she's been fed on nut kernels!' said the old robber woman, who had a long bristly beard and shaggy eyebrows hanging over her eyes. 'She's as tender and sweet as a little fat lamb. Yum, yum! She'll make a tasty dinner!' She drew out a bright sharp knife, which glittered quite dreadfully.

'Ouch!' screeched the hag all at once. She had been bitten in the ear by her own little daughter who hung on her back, and who was so wild and mischievous that she was quite out of hand. 'You loathsome brat!' said her mother, and forgot what she had meant to do with Gerda.

'She shall be my playmate,' said the little robber girl. 'She shall give me her muff and her pretty clothes and sleep with me in my bed.' And so spoilt and wilful was she that of course she had her own way. She got in the coach with Gerda, and away they drove, through bush and briar, deeper and deeper into the forest. The little girl was no taller than Gerda, but much sturdier, with broader shoulders and darker skin. Her eyes were quite black, with a curious look of melancholy in them. She put her arm around little Gerda and said: 'They shan't kill you – not as long as I don't get cross with you. You're a princess, I suppose?'

'No,' said little Gerda, and again she told all her adventures, and how fond she was of little Kay. The robber girl watched her seriously, and nodded her head. 'They shan't kill you even if I do get cross with you,' she said. 'I'll do it myself.' Then she dried Gerda's eyes and put both her hands into the pretty muff which was so soft and warm.

Suddenly the carriage stopped; they had reached the courtyard of a robber's castle. Its walls were cracked from top to bottom; crows and ravens were flying out of the gaps and holes, while huge hounds, each one looking as if he could swallow a man, leapt high into the air; but not a single bark came from them, for that was forbidden. In the great old hall, cobwebbed and black with soot, a large fire burned on the stone floor; the smoke drifted about under the roof, trying to find its own way out. A vast cauldron of soup was bubbling away; hares and rabbits were roasting on turning-spits.

'Tonight you shall sleep with me and all my pets,' said the robber girl. First they had something to eat and drink, then they went over to a corner where straw and blankets were scattered. Above them in holes and on ledges about a hundred pigeons were roosting; they seemed asleep but a slight stir ran through them when the little girls appeared.

'They're mine – all of them,' said the little robber girl. She seized one of the nearest, took it by the legs, and shook it until it flapped its wings. 'Kiss it!' she cried, waving it in Gerda's face. Then she pointed to some wooden bars nailed over a hole above their heads. 'Those are woodland riff-raff, both of them. They'd fly off in a flash if they weren't locked up. And here's my special sweetheart Bae.' She pulled a reindeer forward by the horn; it was tethered to the wall, with a shiny copper ring round its neck. 'He's another one who'd fly off if we didn't keep him prisoner. Every night I tickle his neck with my sharp knife – he doesn't care for that!' And, drawing a long knife out of a crack in the wall, she ran it lightly across the reindeer's neck. The poor creature struggled and kicked, but the robber girl laughed, and pulled Gerda down with her under the rug.

'Are you taking that knife into bed with you?' Gerda asked, as she looked at it nervously.

'I always sleep with a knife at hand,' said the little robber girl. 'You never know what may happen. But now tell me again about little Kay and why you came out into the wide world.' So Gerda told her tale once more, from the very beginning, and the wood-pigeons moaned in their cage, and the other pigeons slept. Then the little robber girl fell asleep too, one arm around Gerda's neck, the other holding the knife; you could hear that she slept from her breathing. But Gerda couldn't even close her eyes, not knowing whether she was to live or die. The robbers sat round the fire and drank and sang, and the robber woman turned somersaults. It was a frightful sight to behold.

Then all at once the wood-pigeons cried: 'Rr-coo! Mmcoo! We have seen little Kay! A white hen was carrying his sledge, and he was sitting in the Snow Queen's carriage which swept low over the forest where we lay in the nest. She breathed down on us young ones and all except the two of us here froze to death. Rr-coo! Mm-coo!'

'What are you saying up there?' cried Gerda. 'Which way did the Snow Queen go? Can you tell me?'

'She must have been making for Lapland, for you'll always find snow and ice there. You ask the reindeer; he's sure to know.'

'Yes, it's a land of ice and snow; everything there is lovely and pleasant,' the reindeer said. 'You can run and leap to your heart's delight in the great shining valleys. There the Snow Queen has her summer palace, but her real home is in a castle far far off towards the North Pole, on an island called Spitzbergen.'

'Oh Kay, poor Kay!' sighed Gerda.

'Lie still, you,' said the robber girl, 'or you'll get my knife in your middle!'

When morning came, Gerda told her all that the wood-pigeons had said. The little robber girl looked very grave, but she nodded and said: 'Never mind – never mind; it's all one . . . Do you know where Lapland is?' she asked the reindeer.

'Who should know better than I?' said the reindeer, and his eyes shone at the thought of it. 'I was born and bred in that land; once I could leap and play freely there in the snowfields.'

'Listen to me,' said the robber girl to Gerda. 'All our menfolk are out. My old Ma's still here and here she'll stay – but later in the morning she'll take a swig from that big bottle and after that she'll have forty winks. Then I'll see what I can do for you.' She jumped out of bed, ran across to her mother, pulled her by the beard and called: 'Good morning, my dear old nanny-goat!' Her mother flipped her on the nose making it quite red and blue – but it was all for sheer affection.

Then, when her mother had had a drink from the bottle and was taking a nap, the robber girl went over to the reindeer. 'I'd love to go on teasing you a few more times with that sharp knife of mine because you always look so funny when I do – but never mind, I'm going to set you free so that you can run to Lapland. But you must put your best foot foremost and take this little girl for me to the Snow Queen's palace where her playmate is. I expect you've heard her story; she was talking loudly enough, and you are always one for eavesdropping.'

The reindeer leapt for joy. The robber girl lifted Gerda on to his back, taking care to tie her firmly on, with a little cushion for a seat.

'You'll be all right,' she said. 'Here are your fur boots – you'll need them in that cold – but I shall keep your muff; it's far too pretty to lose. Still, you won't have to freeze; here are my mother's big gloves. They'll reach right up to your elbows. Shove your hands in! Now they look just like my ugly old mother's!'

Gerda wept with happiness.

'I can't stand that snivelling,' said the little robber girl. 'You ought to be looking really pleased. Here are two loaves and a ham, so you won't starve.' These provisions were tied to the reindeer's back. Then the little robber girl opened the door and called in all the big dogs; after that she cut the rope with her knife and said to the reindeer, 'Off you go! But take good care of the little girl!'

Gerda stretched out her hands in the enormous gloves and called 'Good-bye!' to the robber girl, and the reindeer sped away past bush and briar, through the great forest, over marsh and moor, and the wide plains, as swiftly as he could go. The wolves howled; the ravens screamed; the sky seemed filled with sneezing, crackling noises – schooo, schooo; piff, piff – each time with a glow of red. 'Those are my dear old Northern Lights,' said the reindeer. 'Aren't they beautiful!' Faster and faster he ran, through the night, through the day. The loaves were finished, and so was the ham – and then they were in Lapland.

Part the Sixth: The Lapland Woman and the Finmark Woman

They stopped at a little hut, a wretched place; the roof nearly touched the ground and the door was so low that the family had to get down on all fours to crawl in and out. Nobody was at home except an old Lapp woman, who was frying fish over an oil lamp. The reindeer told her Gerda's story, but first it told its own, which seemed the more important. Gerda was too frozen with cold to speak at all.

'Oh, you poor things!' cried the Lapland woman. 'You've a long way to go yet. You still have several hundred miles to cross before you get to Finmark – that's where the Snow Queen is just now, sending off those fireworks of hers every night. I'll write you a few words on a piece of dried codfish – I've got no paper – and you take it to the Finnwoman living up there. She can tell you better than I can what to do.' And so, when Gerda was properly warm and had had some supper, the Lapland woman wrote some words on a piece of dried cod and told Gerda to take good care of it. Then she fastened her on the reindeer's back again, and off they sped. 'Schooo, schooo! Crack! crack!' came the noises from the sky, and all night long the glorious Northern Lights flashed violet blue. At last they arrived in Finmark and knocked on the Finnwoman's chimney, for she hadn't even a door.

Inside, it was so swelteringly hot that the Finnwoman wore hardly a stitch of clothing. She was small and dumpy, with a brownish skin. The first thing she did was to loosen little Gerda's clothes, and take off her boots and thick gloves; then she laid a piece of ice on the reindeer's head; then studied what was written on the dried-fish letter. She read it three times; after that she knew it by heart, and she dropped it into the cooking pot, for she never wasted anything.

The reindeer now told his story, and after that, little Gerda's; and the Finnwoman's wise eyes twinkled, but she didn't say a word.

'Ah, you're so clever,' said the reindeer. 'I know you can tie up all the winds in the world with a single thread; when the captain undoes the first knot he gets a fair wind; if he undoes the second, then gusts begin to blow; if he undoes the third and fourth, a gale roars up that hurls down the forest trees and wrecks the ship. Won't you make this little girl a magic drink that will give her the strength of twelve men, so that she can overcome the Snow Queen?'

'The strength of twelve men?' said the Finmark woman. 'A lot of good *that* would be!' She went over to a shelf and took down a rolled-up parchment. She opened it out; strange letters were written on it, and she read so intently that the sweat ran from her brow like rain.

But the reindeer went on pleading so hard for little Gerda, and Gerda looked at her with such tearful beseeching eyes, that once again she turned her gaze on them. Then, drawing the reindeer into a corner, she put fresh ice on his head and whispered in his ear:

'Little Kay is with the Snow Queen, sure enough; he finds everything there to his liking, and thinks that he's in the finest place in the world – but all that is because he has a splinter of glass in his heart, and another in his eye. These must come out or he'll stay bewitched, and the Snow Queen will keep her hold over him for ever!'

'But is there nothing that you can give little Gerda to break that hold?'

'I cannot give her greater power than she has already. Don't you see how great that is? How men and beasts all feel that they must serve her? How far she has come in the wide world on her own bare feet? She must not learn of her power; it comes from her own heart, from her being a dear and innocent child. If she can't find her own way into the Snow Queen's palace and free little Kay, there is nothing that we can do to help. Now! About ten miles further north is the edge of the Snow Queen's garden. You can carry the little girl as far as that, then put her down by the big bush with red berries, standing in the snow; don't stay gossiping, but hurry back here.' With that, the Finnwoman lifted little Gerda on to the reindeer's back, and off he dashed as fast as his legs could go.

'Oh! I've left my boots behind! And my gloves!' cried little Gerda. She felt stung by the piercing cold. But the reindeer dared not stop; on he ran till he came to the big bush with the red berries. There he put Gerda down, and kissed her on the lips; as he did so, great shining tears ran down the poor animal's face. Then he turned and sped back as fast as he was able.

And there was poor Gerda, without boots, without gloves, in the midst of that terrible icy land and its piercing cold.

She started to run forward, but a whole regiment of snowflakes appeared in front of her. They had not fallen from above, for the sky was quite clear, sparkling with Northern Lights. These flakes came running along the ground, and the nearer they came the larger they grew. Gerda remembered how strange and wonderfully made the flakes had seemed when she'd looked at them through the magnifying glass. How long ago that was. But these were far bigger and much more frightening – they were the Snow Queen's frontier guards. They had the weirdest, most fantastic shapes. Some were like huge wild hedgehogs; others were like knotted bunches of snakes writhing their heads in all directions; others again were like fat little bears with icicles for hair. All of them were glistening white; all were living snowflakes.

Then little Gerda began to say the Lord's Prayer, and the cold was so intense that she could see her own breath; it rose from her mouth like a cloud. The cloud became thicker and thicker, and took the form of little bright angels who grew in size the moment they touched the ground. On their heads were helmets; in their hands were spears and shields. By the time Gerda had finished her prayer, she was encircled by a whole legion of these spirits. They struck out at the dreadful snow-things, shattering them into hundreds of pieces, and Gerda was able to go on her way without fear or danger. The angels patted her feet and hands so that she hardly felt the biting cold, and she hurried on towards the Snow Queen's palace.

But now we must see how little Kay was faring. Whatever his thoughts, they were not of Gerda;

he certainly did not dream that she was just outside the palace.

Part the Seventh: What Happened at the Snow Queen's Palace, and What Took Place After That

The palace walls were of driven snow, and the doors and windows of cutting wind. There were over a hundred halls, just as the drifting snow had formed them; the largest stretched for miles. All were lit by the brilliant Northern Lights; they were vast, empty, glittering, bleak as ice and deathly cold. In the very midst of the palace there was a frozen lake; it had split into a thousand pieces, but each piece was so exactly like the next that it seemed not an accident but a cunning work of art. The Snow Queen always sat in the centre of this lake whenever she was at home; she used to say that she was on the Mirror of Reason, the best – indeed, the only glass that mattered – in the world.

Little Kay was quite blue with cold; in fact, he was nearly black. But he never noticed, for the Snow Queen had kissed away his shivering and his heart was hardly more than a lump of ice. He was busily dragging about some sharp flat pieces of ice, arranging them in every possible pattern. What he was trying to do was to make a special word, and this he could never manage, try as he would. The word was ETERNITY. For the Snow Queen had said to him: 'If you can spell out *that* for me, you shall be your own master, and I'll make you a present of the whole world, together with a new pair of skates.' But he still could not manage it.

'Now I must fly off to the warm lands,' said the Snow Queen. 'I want to take a peep into the black cauldrons.' (She meant the volcanoes, Etna and Vesuvius.) 'I shall whiten their tops a little; it does them good after all those lemons and grapes.' Off she flew, and Kay was left quite alone in the

vast empty hall, gazing at the pieces of ice, and thinking, thinking, until his head seemed to crack. There he sat, stiff and still; anyone might have thought that he was frozen to death.

It was just then that little Gerda stepped into the palace through the great doors of cutting winds. But she said her evening prayer, and the cold winds dropped as if they were falling asleep. She entered the vast cold empty hall – and there was Kay! She knew him at once; she rushed towards him and flung her arms about his neck and held him tight, crying: 'Kay! dear little Kay! I've found you at last!'

But he sat there quite still, stiff and cold.

Then Gerda began to weep hot tears; they fell on his breast and reached right through to his heart. There, they thawed the lump of ice, and washed away the splinter of glass. Kay looked up at her, and she sang the verse that they used to sing together.

'In the vale the rose grows wild;
Children play all the day –
One of them is the Christ-child.'

Then tears came into Kay's eyes too. And, as he cried, the splinter of glass was washed away; now he could recognize her, and he cried out joyfully:

'Gerda! Dear little Gerda! Where have you been all this time? And what has been happening to me?' He looked around him. 'How cold it is! How huge and empty!' The air was so filled with their happiness that even the pieces of ice began dancing for sheer delight, and when they were tired and lay down again they formed the very word which the Snow Queen had told Kay to make – the one for which he would be his own master, and be given the whole world, and a new pair of skates.

Then Gerda kissed his cheeks, and their colour came back to them; she kissed his eyes, and they shone like hers; she kissed his hands and feet, and he was well and sound, and warm, the Kay she had always known. The Snow Queen could now come back as soon as she liked; Kay's sign of release was there, laid out in shining letters of ice.

Hand in hand, they walked out of the great echoing palace. Wherever they went the winds were still and the sun broke out. When they reached the bush with the red berries, there stood the reindeer, waiting for them. With him was a young doe, and she gave warm milk to the boy and girl. Then the reindeer and the doe carried Kay and Gerda first to the Finmark woman, where they warmed themselves in the hot room and were given advice about the journey home – and then to the Lapland woman. She had made new clothes for them, and had prepared a sledge.

The reindeer and the doe bounded along right up to the borders of their country. There, Kay and Gerda could see the first green shoots of spring coming out of the ground; the sledge could go no further, and the reindeer and the Lapland woman had to return to the north. 'Farewell! Farewell! Good-bye! Good-bye!' said each and all.

The first little birds of spring began to twitter; the first green leaves appeared on the forest trees, and through the wood came a young girl riding a splendid horse. Gerda knew that horse, for it had been harnessed to her golden coach. The young girl had a scarlet cap on her head and pistols at her side. She was the robber girl! She was tired of home life, she told them, and was making for the North; if she did not like it there she would try some other direction. She recognized Gerda at once and Gerda recognized her; they were both delighted to meet each other again.

'You're a fine one to go straying off like that!' she said to Kay. 'I wonder if you deserve to have anyone running to the ends of the earth for your sake!'

But Gerda patted her cheek and asked after the prince and princess.

'They've gone travelling to foreign parts,' said the robber girl.

'And the raven?'

'Oh, the raven's dead,' she replied. 'His tame sweetheart's a widow now and wears a piece of black wool on her leg. She's always moaning and groaning but it doesn't mean a thing. Now you tell me your adventures, and how you managed to find him.' And Gerda and Kay both told their separate tales.

'Well, well, well; today's mishap is tomorrow's story,' said the robber girl. She took each of them by the hand, and promised that if she ever passed through their home town she would pay them a visit. Then she rode off and away, into the wide world.

But Kay and Gerda went on, hand in hand. As they went, the spring flowered round them, beautiful with blossoms and green leaves. They heard the church bells ringing; they saw ahead the towers and walls of a city; they were nearing home.

And they entered the town, and went up the stairs of the grandmother's house, and into the room near the roof, where everything stood just where it was before, and the clock still said 'Tick tock', and the hands still marked the hours. But as they went through the door they noticed that they themselves had grown; they were not young children. The roses in the wooden boxes were flowering in at the open window, and out there were their own little wooden stools. Kay and Gerda sat down on them and held each other's hands. The terrible icy splendour of the Snow Queen's palace had slipped away from their minds like a distant dream. Grandmother sat beside them in the heavenly sunshine and read to them from the Bible:

'Except ye become as little children, ye shall not enter into the Kingdom of Heaven.'

Kay and Gerda looked into each other's eyes, and at once they remembered the old song, and saw its meaning:

'In the vale the rose grows wild;
Children play all the day –
One of them is the Christ-child'

So there they sat together, the same children still at heart. And it was summer, warm delightful summer . . .

The Shepherdess and the Chimney Sweep

Have you ever seen a very old cupboard or cabinet, quite black with age, carved all over with trailing stems and leaves?

There was a cabinet of this kind in a sitting-room; once it had belonged to the family's great-great-grandmother. It was covered from top to bottom with carvings of roses and tulips, surrounded by curly flourishes, while through the spaces, numbers of little carved deer poked out their antlered heads.

But in the middle there was the complete figure of a man – well, of an odd sort of character. He was comical enough to look at, for he had legs like a goat's, small horns coming out of his forehead, a long beard and a peculiar sort of grin – you could hardly call it a smile. The children of the house called him Brigadier-Majorgeneral-Captain-

Sergeant-Corporal-Goatlegs; the name suited him, they thought, because it was hard to say. Besides, who else, living or carved, ever deserved such a title?

Anyhow, there he was, and his eyes were turned all the time to the table under the mirror, for on the table stood a lovely little china shepherdess. Her shoes were gilt; her dress was neatly pinned with a china rose. She also had a golden hat and she held a shepherd's crook. Oh, she was beautiful!

Close beside her was a little chimney sweep; he too was made of china. All of him was black except his face, which was pink and white as a girl's; really, he was just as clean and tidy as anyone else, for he was only a make-believe sweep.

The china-maker could have turned him out just as well as a prince. And there he stood, with his ladder and his pretty face which hadn't even a dab of soot on it. And since the sweep and the shepherdess had always been placed together on the table, they became engaged; the most natural thing in the world. Indeed, they were very well suited. Both were young, both were made of the same kind of china clay; each was quite as fragile as the other.

Not far away was a very different figure, about three times their size. This was an old Chinaman, a mandarin, who could nod his head. He too was made of china and he always declared that he was the shepherdess's grandfather. He could give no proof but he insisted that he was her guardian, so, when Majorgeneral-Goatlegs asked for her hand in marriage, he nodded his consent.

'There's a fine husband for you,' he said to the shepherdess. 'He is made of mahogany – I am almost sure of it – and you will become Madam-Lady-Brigadier-Majorgeneral-Captain-Sergeant-Corporal-Goatlegs. He owns this whole cupboard full of silver plate, as well as what he has secretly hidden away.'

'I don't want to go into that dark cupboard,' said the little shepherdess. 'I've heard that he has eleven china wives in there already.'

'Then you can be the twelfth,' said the Mandarin. 'Tonight, as soon as the cupboard starts creaking, the wedding will take place, as sure as I'm a

Chinaman!' With that, he nodded his head and went to sleep.

But the little shepherdess began to cry and look at her true love, the chimney sweep. 'I think I must ask you,' she said, 'to come out into the wide world with me, for we cannot stay here.'

'Your will is my will,' said the little chimney sweep. 'Let us start at once; I feel sure that I can earn enough to keep you by my profession.'

'Oh, if only we were down from the table,' she said. 'I cannot be happy until we are out in the wide world.'

So he comforted her, and showed her where to place her little foot on the carved projections and the gilded leaves down the leg of the table. He took his ladder, too, to help her, and there they were at least on the floor. But when they looked up at the dark old cupboard – what a commotion! All the carved deer were poking out their heads still further, pricking their antlers, turning their necks from side to side. And Brigadier-Majorgeneral-Captain-Sergeant-Corporal-Goat-legs was jumping up and down, and shouting across to the old Chinaman, 'They're running away! They're running away!'

This frightened the lovers, and they quickly hid in the drawer of the window seat. Here they found three or four packs of cards – none of them quite complete – and a little toy theatre. A play was being acted, and all the card queens –

diamonds, hearts, clubs and spades – were sitting in the front row, fanning themselves with their tulips. Behind them stood all the knaves, with their two heads, one at the top, one at the bottom; all playing-cards are like that. The play they were watching was about two lovers who were prevented from marrying. And the shepherdess wept again, for it was just her own story.

'I cannot bear it,' she said. 'I must get out of this drawer.'

But when they had reached the ground and looked up at the table, the old Chinaman had awakened, and was rocking his body to and fro; he had to move like this, since – apart from his head – he was made all in one piece.

'The old Chinaman is coming!' shrieked the little shepherdess, and so terrified was she that she fell down on her porcelain knees.

'I have an idea,' said the chimney sweep. 'Let us creep into the big pot-pourri jar over there in the corner; we can hide in there among the roses and lavender, and throw salt in his eyes if he comes.'

'That will not help,' she said. 'Besides, I happen to know that the old Chinaman and the pot-pourri jar were once engaged; and there is always some feeling left when people have been as close as that. No, there's nothing left for us but to go forth into the wide world.'

'Have you really the courage to come with me into the wide world?' asked the chimney sweep.

'Do you realize how vast it is? And that we can never come back again?'

'Yes, I have thought of that,' she answered.

The chimney sweep gave her a keen and serious look. Then he said:

'The only path I know lies through the chimney. Are you sure you are brave enough to follow me through the heart of the stove, and into the dark tunnel of the flue? That is the way to the chimney, and once I am there I shall know how to manage. We shall climb so high that no one can reach us – and, right at the top, there's a hole that leads out into the wide world.'

And he led her across to the door of the stove.

'It looks very black,' she said. But she went with him all the same, through firebrick and flue, where the darkness was black as night.

'Now we are in the chimney,' he said. 'And, look! The loveliest star is shining over our heads!'

Yes, there was indeed a real star in the sky overhead, shining right down on them as though it wanted to show them the way. On they clambered, on they crawled, up and up and up, higher and higher; it was a horrible journey. But the little sweep kept lifting and helping her, showing her the best places for putting her little china feet, until at last they arrived at the edge of the chimney pot; there they sat down, for they were tired out, and no wonder.

High above was the sky with all its stars; below was the town with all its roofs. They could see

far, far around them, where the wide world lay with its distances. The poor shepherdess had never imagined anything like it; she laid her little head on the sweep's shoulder and cried so bitterly that the gold was washed from her sash.

'It is all too much,' she cried. 'I cannot bear it. The world is too big. Oh, if only I were back again on the table under the mirror! I shall never be happy until I am there again. I have followed you into the wide world; now, if you really care for me, I beg you to take me home again.'

The chimney sweep gently reasoned with her; he reminded her of the Chinaman, and of Brigadier-Majorgeneral-Captain-Sergeant-Corporal-Goatlegs – but she wept with despair and kissed and clung to her chimney sweep until he could not help giving in to her, foolish as it was.

So they crawled back down the chimney – a hard and perilous business – and crept through the flue (one of the nastiest parts of the journey), and at last they found themselves inside the dark cavern of the stove. They stood behind its door for a while to hear what was going on in the room. Everything seemed quiet enough, so they peeped out – but oh! There in the middle of the floor lay the old Chinaman! Trying to run after them, he had fallen from his table, and now he lay broken into three pieces – his back, his front, and his head, which had rolled into a corner. The Brigadier-Majorgeneral-Captain-Sergeant-Corporal-Goatlegs stood fixed where he had always stood, deep in thought.

'How terrible!' cried the little shepherdess. 'Old grandfather is broken to bits, and it is all our fault. I shall never get over it!' And she wrung her little hands.

'He can still be mended,' said the chimney sweep. 'That can easily be done. Now don't get so excited. When they have glued him together and put a rivet in his neck he'll be as good as new – he'll be able to say plenty of tiresome things to us yet.'

'Do you think so?' she said. And they climbed back to the table-top where they stood before.

'Well, we have been a long way,' said the chimney sweep, 'and here we are back where we started. We might have spared ourselves the journey.'

'Oh, if only old grandfather were mended!' the shepherdess said. 'Will it cost very much, do you think?'

The Chinaman *was* mended. The family had his back glued on; a rivet was put in his neck, and he looked as good as new – but he could no longer nod his head.

'You *have* become high and mighty since you were broken!' said Brigadier-Majorgeneral-Captain-Sergeant-Corporal-Goatlegs. 'But what have you got to be proud of? Tell me, am I to have the shepherdess or not?'

The sweep and the shepherdess looked anxiously at the old Chinaman, for they were afraid that he might nod. But he could not do this, and he did not wish to admit that he had a rivet in his neck. So the little porcelain lovers stayed together, and went on loving each other in the greatest happiness until they broke.

The Happy Family

The biggest green leaf we have in this country is certainly the burdock leaf. A little girl could wear it as an apron; if she put it over her head in rainy weather, it would be as good as an umbrella – that's how big it is. No burdock ever grows alone; no, where one grows, there are plenty of others. They make a splendid show – and all that splendour used to be food for snails. A special kind of large white snail lives on the leaves, a kind of snail that rich people used to have made into a fricassée. They would murmur, 'Delicious!' as they ate it. That is why the burdocks came to be planted.

Now, there was an old manor house where they had long given up eating snails. The snails had almost died out, but not the burdocks – these grew and multiplied. They spread all over the paths and flower beds till they were quite out of hand – the garden was an absolute burdock forest. Here and there stood an apple tree or plum tree; otherwise you would never have known that it was a garden. Burdocks were everywhere – and among these lived the last two surviving snails, both extremely old.

They did not know, themselves, how old they were, but they could well remember that there had once been many more of them, that their family came from foreign parts, and that it was for them and theirs that the whole vast burdock forest had been planted. They had never been outside it, though they *did* know that there was one more thing in the world, called the manor house. There, you were *cooked*, and you turned black, and were placed on a silver dish; but what happened after that, no one knew. For that matter, they could not imagine what it felt like to be cooked and put on a silver dish, but it was supposed to be most interesting, and was certainly very distinguished. The cockchafer, toad and earthworm were questioned about it, but none of these could help, for none of them had ever been cooked or placed on a silver dish.

The old white snails were the aristocrats of the world – they had no doubts about that. The forest existed just for them and so did the ancient manor house and its silver dish.

They passed their days in a quiet, secluded happiness, and as they had no children they had adopted a little common snail which they brought up as their own. The little thing grew no bigger, for he was just a common snail. Yet the old folk, especially Mother Snail, always thought that he had grown a bit since yesterday. And when Father Snail seemed not to see the difference, she would ask him to feel the little shell. And so he would feel it, and agree that Mother was right.

One day there was a heavy rainstorm. 'Listen to the drum-drum-drum on the burdock leaves!' said Father Snail.

'Yes, and some of the drops are coming through,' said Mother Snail. 'Look, they are running right down the stalks. My goodness, it's going to be wet down here! How thankful I am for our good houses – a personal one for each, and for our little one, too! Really, we must be the most favoured creatures! It's plain enough that we are the princes of the world. We each have a house as soon as we are born, and a whole forest planted for our benefit. I do wonder sometimes how far it stretches, and what there is beyond it.'

'There is nothing beyond it,' replied Father. 'No one can be better off anywhere than here, and I don't want to look any further.'

'Oh, but I do,' said Mother Snail. 'I *would* rather like to go to the manor and be cooked – whatever that is – and laid on the silver dish. All our ancestors have done so which shows that there must be something special about it.'

'The manor house may have fallen into ruins by now,' said Father Snail. 'Or it may be overgrown with burdocks, so that the people in it can't come out. Anyhow, there is no need to be in such a hurry. You are always in such a rush, rush, rush, and now the little one is starting too. In three days he has nearly finished crawling up that stalk; it makes me quite giddy to look at him.'

'Now don't complain of our boy,' said Mother Snail. 'He crawls along so carefully! I'm sure he'll be a great joy to us – and after all, what else have we old folks to live for? But have you thought of where we can find a wife for him? Don't you think that, somewhere deep in this forest of burdocks, there might be one of our own kind?'

'Well, I daresay there are plenty of slugs and such, that go about without a house of their own,' said the old Father. 'But that would be a comedown for us, though they do give themselves airs. Still, we might commission the ants to look about. They are always scurrying to and fro as if they had plenty to do; they might very well know of a wife for our little snail.'

'Ah, yes,' said the ants, 'we know the most beautiful bride; but it might be hard to arrange, for she is a queen.'

'That wouldn't matter,' said the old snail. 'But has she a house?'

'She has a palace,' replied the ants, 'a magnificent ant palace with seven hundred corridors.'

'Thank you!' said Mother Snail. 'Our son is not going into an ant-hill! If that's the best you can do, we'll pass on our inquiry to the white gnats; they fly far and wide in rain or sun; they know our forest inside and out.'

'Yes, we have a wife for him,' said the midges. 'A hundred man-paces from here, on a gooseberry bush, is a little snail with a house. She is quite alone, and is old enough to marry. It's only a hundred man-paces away.'

'Well,' said the old couple, 'let her come to him. He owns a whole burdock forest; she has only a bush!'

So the gnats went and fetched the little snail maiden. It took eight days to make the journey, but that did not displease the parents; it showed that she came of good snail family.

And so the wedding took place. Six glow-worms did their best to provide the lighting, otherwise the affair was quiet enough, for the old snails did not care for feasting and merrymaking. But Mother Snail made a charming speech – Father was too overcome to speak himself. And then they handed over the whole dock forest to the young couple, saying, as they had always said, that it was the best place in the world, and that if the young pair lived honest respectable lives, and had plenty of children, they and their family might some day go to the manor house and be 'cooked', whatever that meant, and laid on a silver dish.

After the speech was over, the old snails retired into their houses, and came out no more. They slept. The two young ones reigned in the forest and had many children; but they were never cooked, nor laid on a silver dish, so they concluded that the manor house had fallen down, and that all the people in the world had died out. And as nobody contradicted them, it must have been true. And the rain beat down on the burdock leaves to make music for them, and the sun shone to brighten the forest with colour, and they were very happy; the whole family was happy; never was there a happier family, you may be sure of that.

The Goblin at the Grocer's

There was once a student, a proper student; he lived in an attic and owned nothing at all. There was also a grocer, a proper grocer; he lived on the ground floor and owned the whole house. And so it was with the grocer that the goblin chose to make his home. Besides, every Christmas he was given a bowl of porridge with a great lump of butter in it. The grocer could manage that easily, and so the goblin stayed in the shop. There's a moral there somewhere, if you look for it.

One evening the student came in through the back door to buy some candles and cheese. His shopping was quickly done and paid for, and the grocer and his wife nodded 'Good evening'. The wife could do more than nod, though; she was a chatterbox – talk, talk, talk. She had what they call the gift of the gab, no doubt about that. The student nodded back – and then his eye fell on something written on the paper wrapping the cheese, and he stood there reading it. It was a page torn from an old book, one which should never have been torn up at all, an old book full of poetry.

'There's more of that book if you want it,' said the grocer. 'I gave an old woman some coffee beans for it. You can have the rest for sixpence if you like.'

'Thank you,' said the student. 'Let me have it instead of the cheese. I can do very well with bread. It's a shame to use such a book for wrapping paper! You are an excellent man, a practical man – but you have no more idea of poetry than that tub over there.'

Now this was a rude thing to say, especially the part about the tub; but the grocer laughed, and the student laughed; after all, it was only a kind of joke. But the little goblin was annoyed that anyone should dare to speak like that to the grocer – his landlord too – an important person who owned the whole house and sold the best quality butter.

That night, when the shop was shut and everyone but the student had gone to bed, the goblin tiptoed in and borrowed the grocer's wife's gift of the gab, for she had no need of it while she was asleep. Then, whatever object he put it on in the room was able to voice its views and opinions quite as well as the lady herself. But only one thing at a time could have it, and that was a blessing; otherwise they would all have been chattering away at once.

First, the goblin placed the gift of the gab on the tub where the old newspapers were kept. 'Is it really true,' he asked, 'that you don't know what poetry is?'

'Of course I know!' said the tub. 'It's something you find at the bottom of the page in a newspaper; people cut it out. I rather think that I have more poetry in me than the student has – yet I'm only a humble tub compared with the grocer.'

Then the goblin placed the gift of the gab on the coffee mill. Goodness, how it clattered on! After that he put it on the butter-cask, then the cash-till. They all echoed the views of the tub, and the views of the majority have to be respected.

'Now I can put that student in his place,' said the goblin, and he tiptoed softly up the back staircase to the attic where the student lived. There was a light inside, and the goblin peeped through the keyhole and saw the young man reading the tattered book from the shop.

But how bright it was in the room! Out of the book rose a shining beam of light; it became a tree-stem, the trunk of a noble tree that soared up and spread its branches over the student. The leaves were fresh and green, and every flower was the face of a lovely girl; some had dark mysterious eyes, some had eyes of sparkling blue. Every fruit was a shining star, and the air was filled with an indescribably beautiful sound of singing.

The little goblin had never seen or known of such wonders; he could never have imagined them, even. And so he stayed at the door, standing on tiptoe, peeping in, gazing and gazing, until the light in the room went out. The student must have blown out his candle and gone to bed – but still the goblin could not tear himself away; his head rang with the marvellous music, which still echoed in the air, lulling the student to sleep.

'This is beyond belief,' said the goblin to himself. 'I certainly never expected anything of the kind. I think I shall stay in the attic with the student.' And then he pondered a while, and then he sighed. 'One must be sensible,' he said. 'The student hasn't any porridge.'

And so – yes – he went down again to the grocer's shop. It was a good thing he did, because the tub had nearly worn out the gift of the gab, what with telling everyone all the news and views of the papers stacked inside. It had done so from one angle, and was just about to turn over and gabble it all again from another, when the goblin took the gab back to the sleeping wife. And from that time the whole shop, from the cash-till to the firewood, took all their opinions from the tub; they held it in such respect that, ever after, when the grocer was reading out criticisms of plays or books from the newspapers, they thought that he had learnt it all from the tub.

But the goblin could no longer sit quietly listening to all the wisdom and good sense that was uttered down in the shop. No – the moment the light began to shine through the attic door, he seemed to be drawn there by powerful strings, and up he had to go and station himself at the keyhole. And each time that he did this, a sense of unutterable grandeur would sweep through him – the kind of feeling that we might have at the sight of a stormy sea whose waves are so wild that God himself might be riding over them in the blast. How wonderful it would be to sit under the tree with the student! But that could never be.

Meanwhile, he was grateful to have the keyhole. He gazed through it every night, standing there on the bleak landing even when the autumn winds blew through the skylight, making him nearly freeze with cold. Yet he felt nothing of this until the light went out in the attic room and the music faded away in the howling of the wind. Brrr! Then he would realize how cold he was, and would creep down again to his secret corner of the shop where it was so snug and warm. Soon there would be the Christmas bowl of porridge with its great lump of butter. Yes – the grocer was the one to choose after all.

But late one night the goblin was woken up by a frightful commotion. People were banging at the shutters; the watchman was blowing his whistle; a fire had broken out, and the whole street seemed ablaze. Which house was burning? This one or the next? Where *was* the fire? What screams! What panic! What a fuss! The grocer's wife was so flustered that she took her gold earrings from her ears and put them in her pocket, so that she might at least save *some*thing. The grocer dashed after his bonds, the maid after the silk shawl that she

had bought with her wages. Everyone ran to collect the thing he or she prized most highly.

And the little goblin did so too. In a bound or two he was up the stairs and in the room of the student, who was standing quite calmly at the open window, looking out at the fire in the house across the road. The goblin seized the wonderful book from the table, put it in his scarlet cap, and hugged it with both arms. The most precious thing in the house was saved! Then he rushed up to the roof, right to the top of the chimney stack, and there he sat, lit up by the flames of the house on fire over the way, still firmly clasping the red cap with the treasure inside.

Now he knew where his heart lay; student? – grocer? – his choice was clear.

But when the fire had been put out, and the goblin had had time to think more calmly – well . . .

'I'll divide my time between them,' he decided. 'I can't quite give up the grocer, because of the porridge.'

Just like a human, really. We too like to keep on good terms with the grocer, because of the porridge.

Dance, Dolly, Dance

'Oh, it's just a silly little song for very small children,' declared Aunt Malle. 'With the best will in the world, I can see no sense in this "Dance, dance, dolly mine". Fribble! Nonsense!'

But little Amalie saw plenty of sense in it. She was only three years old; but she knew how to play with dolls, and she was bringing hers up to be as clever as Aunt Malle.

A student came regularly to the house; he helped the brothers with their homework and he talked a great deal with little Amalie and her dolls. Nobody else spoke to Amalie as he did. He made her laugh, he was so funny and teasing. But he never made fun of her, and he spoke of important things that they both understood.

Aunt Malle insisted that he didn't know how to treat children at all; their little heads couldn't possibly take in all his ridiculous nonsense. But little Amalie's could; in fact, she learnt the whole of the student's ditty by heart and sang it to her three dolls. Two of them were new; one was a girl, one a boy. The third was last year's doll; her name was Lisa. Lisa listened to the song – indeed, she was in it!

'Dance, my dolly, dance away!
What a treat she looks today!
Her boy-doll friend is handsome too,
In trousers white and jacket blue,
Hat and gloves – oh, what a beau!
Shoes so smart they pinch his toe –
He is fine and she is fine.
Dance, dance, dolly mine.

This *one's Lisa from last year,*
But she'll dance without a care.
See, her flaxen hair is new!
Freshly washed, her face shines too –
Why, she *could be the youngest one.*
Good old Lisa! Join the fun.
Twirl and leap! It's worth a fee
Just to watch my dollies three.

Dance, my dollies, neat and light;
You know the steps so get them right.
Point your toe and don't forget
How to do a pirouette;
Curtsy nicely, turn and bow
Just as I have taught you how.
You're Amalie's pride and joy,
Her dolly girls, her dolly boy.'

Well, the dolls understood the song; little Amalie understood it; the student understood it too. After all, he had written it himself, and *he* said it was excellent. Only Aunt Malle did not understand it – but then, she had climbed out of the country of childhood such a long time ago. Aunt Malle might call the song nonsense but not so Amalie. She goes on singing it.

It is from her singing that we have it here.

Notes

The first four of Andersen's tales appeared in a small booklet in May 1835, and the second three in December 1835. Thereafter a few more were published year by year until almost the end of his life. There were 156 in all.

The Princess and the Pea

This fine brisk piece of storytelling was one of the opening four (see above) in the booklet of May 1835. Like a few of the earliest tales, it is based on a folk tale that Andersen heard as a child from local peasant women 'either in the spinning room or during the gathering of hops'. What is a real princess (or prince)? Sometimes Andersen answered this one way, sometimes in another. He himself had risen from the lowest rank, but he had a high regard for royalty, if not for courtiers. (In one late story, 'Everything in Its Place', the blast of a certain whistle sorts high and low, rich and poor, into their true social positions, with very odd results.)

Some early translators thought that one pea was ridiculous and made it several. Be warned if you come across one of these versions!

Thumbelina

Another very early story, this first appeared in December 1835, in the second little collection. Old fairy tales, in every part of the world, tell of children who have magically grown (like Thumbelina) from flowers, barley grains and such. But every detail shows this to be a true Andersen story. Though the scale is so small that a walnut shell can be the tiny heroine's bed, a rose petal her cover, and a wintry stubble field can seem a terrible forest, her story could be any human story. The 'warm countries' had a special meaning for Andersen, who had just made his own first Italian journey from the bleakness of the North. Perhaps he is needlessly hard on toad and mole and mouse; some later writers have done better for these small creatures. Can you find Andersen in the tale? He is unmistakably there, at the end.

The Emperor's New Clothes

Another of the very early stories, this first appeared (with 'The Little Mermaid' – a wonderful pair!) in the third published booklet, early in 1837. They were the eighth and ninth of the tales. Andersen notes that the idea of the cheats came from a medieval Spanish tale told by a Prince Don Juan Manuel, which he had found in a recent German version. But that was just a crude anecdote, nothing like the witty and memorable short story that we have now. An odd and little-known fact is that the ending, about the child, was a last-minute inspiration. In his original manuscript the ending runs: '"I must put on that suit whenever I appear in a public procession or before a gathering of people," said the Emperor, and since nobody wished to seem stupid, everyone praised the wonderful new clothes.' As soon as the tale had gone to the printer's, Andersen thought again, and had the ending changed to the one we know. Indeed, this brings home the real point of the story – that people are too ready to accept what they think they *ought* to believe (or what everyone else seems to believe) instead of taking a stand for themselves. And a very important point it is.

The Little Mermaid

First published in 1837 (see note above), this striking early story made such an impact that Andersen himself began to realize the immense range and possibilities of his new form of writing. A few years earlier he had written a verse drama called 'Agnete and the Merman'; Matthew Arnold's 'Forsaken Merman', written later, has much the same plot. But the new fairy tale contained much more of Andersen himself, both as the story of an 'outsider' (which he still felt himself to be), and as a tale of unrequited love, which again was his own experience at this time. It stands out for other reasons. Few fairy tales have ever had such a marvellous opening; few fairy tales have such a pervading sense of the sea, in calm, in storm – especially in the scenes where each mermaid comes in turn to the surface. Reading, we seem ourselves to belong in these deep waters, to have no fear at all in the towering waves; the land and its human people seem by contrast vague and remote. The story has always been popular, and the setting up of the mermaid statue in 1913 on a rock outside Copenhagen has kept it in passers' minds.

For all this, the tale has a flaw. It leaves us with a sense of unfairness, which Andersen's father would have been quick to notice. Why should the pleasant but somewhat stupid prince and his raffish, idle followers have their undeserved heaven-advantage over the mermaid heroine, the only one to show anything like a 'soul'? Not so long since, and in parts of the world still, not only mermaids and fairies but women, the dark-skinned, the illiterate poor, the blind, the deaf and other underprivileged human groups have been thought to lack the soul possessed by more substantial persons. Today, this wilful distinction is used to justify every form of cruelty practised on the non-human *animal* kind. The old inherited superstition in Andersen rising up! You might find it interesting to read, after this, Oscar Wilde's remarkable story 'The Fisherman and his Soul' which reverses the situation. Wilde owed much to Andersen, but the two tales are well worth comparing.

The Steadfast Tin Soldier

First published in 1838, this was one of the first tales to tell a human drama through non-human things, such as toys and kitchen-stuff. A special piece of Andersen invention, it was to inspire a long line of children's stories; Hoban's 'The Mouse and His Child' is one of the best of its modern descendants. Robert Louis Stevenson knew this tale when he wrote his own haunting tin-soldier poem in *A Child's Garden of Verses*. Various people told Andersen that the story of the one-legged soldier, enduring so many trials and rebuffs, gave them courage in their own experiences. Is the ending happy or sad? I don't think that Andersen means it to be an unhappy one. The soldier keeps his dauntless spirit; he even, however strangely, gets his wish. The tale is full of personal details – the cut-out paper dancer, the paper castle, the passport too. Andersen was always having to produce one on his travels and always feared that he'd lost it.

The Nightingale

On 11 October 1843, Andersen wrote in his diary: 'Began the Chinese story.' He worked fast, as he often did on his finest works; the result, 'The Nightingale', was published the following month with two other tales, one of which was 'The Ugly Duckling'. Why is this set in China? One clue can be found in his autobiography. As a child, he recalls,

> An old woman rinsing out clothes in the Odense river told me that the Empire of China lay directly underneath. I did not think it impossible that a Chinese prince, on some moonlit night, might dig himself up through the earth; hearing me sing he would take me down to his kingdom, make me rich and noble, and then let me return to Odense. There I would live in style and build myself a castle. I spent many evenings working out the plans for this.

Andersen as a young boy had a very sweet singing voice; local people sometimes called him 'the little nightingale'. But of course many other elements went to make the tale. One was Andersen's love for the singer Jenny Lind, the 'Swedish nightingale', who was visiting Copenhagen in 1843. She was still not widely known outside Sweden, and fashionable audiences were giving more attention to an Italian opera group at the Court Theatre. But Andersen too was an unworldly bird who won the heart of princes. The great ending passage, where the bird wins the Emperor's life from Death, comes from nowhere but Andersen's genius.

The Ugly Duckling

First published late in 1843 (in the same booklet as 'The Nightingale') this is probably the best-known Andersen tale in any part of the world, even by people who have no idea who wrote the story. The idea came to him in the summer of 1842, when he was staying at Gisselfeldt, one of the great manors of the Danish aristocracy. As he wandered through the woods, in very low spirits, the thought of what he then called 'The Story of a Duck' suddenly flashed into his mind, and cheered his melancholy. Three weeks later, as guest in the manor of Bregentved, he noted: 'Began "The Cygnet" yesterday.' It was six months before he finished it; most of his tales sped along more quickly.

'The Ugly Duckling' is of course Andersen's own life story. But it has meaning too for almost every reader; is there anyone who does not at some time feel misunderstood, under-valued? Another feature of the tale is worth noticing; as you read, you journey through the Danish countryside, ending (where the bird is revealed as a swan) in the grounds of one of those manors where the idea first came to Andersen. There are many accounts of his reading this story aloud. One such occasion was at a house party in Rome, where he read it in rather poor English to the children. Browning (who was also there) did better, immediately after, with the 'Pied Piper'.

The Snow Queen [*See also Introduction*]

This is Andersen's masterpiece, and in some ways unlike anything else he ever wrote. Yet we know less about its making than we do about almost any other of his best-known tales. Long as it is, it was written fast. We are told that it was begun on 5 December 1844, and was – incredibly – published in book form on 21 December. This, as a feat of writing and printing, seems hardly possible; but he did say, in a letter to the Danish writer Ingemann: 'It has been sheer joy for me to put on paper my most recent tale "The Snow Queen". It took hold of my mind in such a way that it came dancing out over the paper.'

So much can be said about this marvellous story. On its own scale it belongs in the great line of quest-stories, a line going further back than Malory of the Arthurian knights, and further on in our time than Tolkien and Le Guin – a perilous journey through unknown paths in search of some one or some thing. The best of all stories, old or new, adult's or children's, are often on this theme.

One thing that makes 'The Snow Queen' differ from almost all other fairy tales is that every positive character is a girl or woman: Gerda herself, the grand-mother, the witch, the princess, the robber girl, the Lapland and Finmark women, the Snow Queen her-self, while the victim to be rescued is, for once, a boy.

Yet all are such individuals in their own right that most readers never perceive this at all, which is as it should be. Unusually for Andersen, 'The Snow Queen', with all its terrible thrills and wonders, is never a sad or mournful story. Even the witch is an amiable old soul, who practises magic only for her own amusement. As for the Queen, with her magical beauty, power and style, she's of a quality that transcends evil; Gerda and Kay can escape but not destroy her, and this seems right.

For once the author himself is hard to find exactly; but a few autobiographical details are of interest. The raven, Andersen tells us, was based on the housekeeper at the Odense royal castle, known to him as a boy. The boy-suitor's creaking shoes go back to a new pair worn by the young Hans Christian; he enjoyed their noise in church because it showed that the shoes *were* new. As for the little roof-garden of herbs and roses, this keeps alive his own mother's roof-box of chives and parsley – the only garden (he tells us) that she ever possessed. 'In my story, "The Snow Queen", that garden flourishes still.'

The Shepherdess and the Chimney Sweep

This brilliantly told little tale was first published in 1845, not long after 'The Snow Queen' and other notable writings – a high time for Andersen's invention. A witty and charming love story it is also one of his best examples of a drama told through things – furniture, ornaments and china figures. The characters are very shrewdly observed – none more so than the lovers themselves. The shepherdess, who insists on escaping and then cannot face the outside world and insists on returning, has nothing in common with Gerda or the robber girl but she is as true to life as they are, nonetheless.

The Happy Family

'In the gardens of Glorup Castle on the island of Fyn, where I used to spend several weeks in the summer,' Andersen recalled, 'the grounds were completely overgrown with giant dock or burdock weeds. These had been planted in bygone times as food for the great white snails which once had been considered a delicacy.' But that was long ago; and now, in this tale, the dock-leaves cover the paths and flower-beds, while the snails themselves have gone, all but two, the very last of the line. Glorup was one of the Danish great estates where Andersen, after he became famous, was a regular visitor. But though the idea of the story came to him here, it was actually written on his first visit to London in 1847, while he was staying in a Leicester Square hotel. It was one of a group of five tales that he arranged to have published *first* in England as a kind of Christmas greeting and tribute to his English friends. Though the manuscript did not arrive at the printers until 15 December 1847, the little collection was actually published less than a fortnight later, between Christmas and New Year. Fast work! Danish publication followed a few weeks later, early in 1848.

Andersen was often to write of people (in the guise of animals, plants, toys and household things) who thought that their own home area was the whole of the world and its customs not to be questioned. (See too 'The Ugly Duckling'.) In his own small country he was often amused or vexed by this view – not that it didn't exist anywhere else! But the happy note of this original little story – part comedy, part fairy tale – makes it shine among his work. His happiness during the London visit had left its mark. If we don't at once notice the wonderfully-held slow snail-pace of the events, this is because we ourselves become part of the scene as soon as we enter it.

The Goblin at the Grocer's

First published in 1853 (the 65th of the stories) this is less well known than some, but admirers of Andersen rank it among the very best of his shorter tales. The little goblin was in fact a 'nisse', a Danish or Norwegian house spirit of the pixie or brownie kind. The poor student with his radiant book of poems is, of course, one view of Andersen. But he is also the goblin trying to choose between the poetry and the porridge. Not only goblins but the rest of us may have to make a choice of this kind. The story also shows, in the fire episode, the absurdity behind many human decisions. If *you* had to save one possession at five minutes' notice, would you know which to choose?

Dance, Dolly, Dance

This charming little piece, first published in 1871, is one of the last that Andersen wrote. It should be new to most readers, for although it can be found in the complete collected edition, it has never appeared before, I believe, in any selection of Andersen's tales in English. No one will have any trouble, I hope, in finding the author himself in the story.

PUFFIN CLASSICS

GRIMMS' FAIRY TALES

From the land of fantastical castles, vast lakes and deep forests, the Brothers Grimm collected a treasury of entrancing folk and fairy stories full of giants and dwarfs, witches and princesses, magic beasts and cunning boys. From favourites such as 'The Frog-Prince' and 'Hansel and Gretel' to the delights of 'Ashputtel' or 'Old Sultan', all are vivid with timeless mystery.

ENGLISH FAIRY TALES

Joseph Jacobs

A 'fairy tale' in this anthology is one in which something extraordinary appears – whether a giant or a speaking animal. So as well as classic stories of magic, like 'Cap o' Rushes', 'Jack and the Beanstalk' and 'Childe Rowland', here are 'The Three Little Pigs' and 'Henny-Penny', and also rarely told gems such as 'Mr Miacca', 'Molly Whuppie' and 'Master of All Masters'.

The Happy Prince and Other Stories

Oscar Wilde

These special fairy tales, which Oscar Wilde made up for his own sons, include 'The Happy Prince', who was not as happy as he seemed; 'The Selfish Giant', who learned to love little children; 'The Star Child', who suffered bitter trials when he rejected his parents ... Often whimsical and sometimes sad, they all shine with poetry and magic.

Tales of Ancient Egypt

Roger Lancelyn Green

These stories include the great myths – of Amen-Ra, who created all the creatures in the world; of Isis, searching the waters for her dead husband Osiris; of the Bennu Bird and the Book of Thoth. But there are also tales told for pleasure, about magic, treasure and adventure – even the first ever Cinderella story.

JUST SO STORIES

Rudyard Kipling

From the 'satiable curiosity of the elephant's child to the crab who played with the sea, from the ingenious invention of the alphabet to how the rhinoceros got his wrinkled skin, these stories of strange happenings in the High and Far-Off Times brim with life, humour and magic – a wonderful collection that will hold you spellbound!

WUTHERING HEIGHTS

Emily Brontë

Heathcliff, a waif found on the streets of Liverpool, is brought home to the Yorkshire moors by Mr Earnshaw and raised as one of his own children. Hindley despises and ill-treats him, but wild Cathy becomes his constant companion, and he falls violently in love with her. When she will not marry him, Heathcliff's terrible vengeance ruins them all – but still his and Cathy's love will not die ...

The Great Adventures of Sherlock Holmes

Sir Arthur Conan Doyle

From the strange case of 'The Red-Headed League' to the extraordinary tale of 'The Engineer's Thumb', Sherlock Holmes and his assistant Dr Watson grapple with treachery, murder, and ingenious crimes of all kinds. But no case is too challenging, no mystery unsolvable, for the immortal detective's unique powers of deduction.

The Mysterious Adventures of Sherlock Holmes

Sir Arthur Conan Doyle

Sherlock Holmes, the great genius of detection, with his assistant Dr Watson, once more attempts to solve the unsolvable. From the extraordinary case of 'The Resident Patient' to the sinister tale of 'The Crooked Man', Holmes unravels the most challenging of mysteries. Using his astounding methods of deduction, he outwits the most cunning of thieves and most villainous of murderers.

